A Handbook
for
Secretaries
of Co-operatives

by Peter Cockerton

ICOM Co-Publications

ICOM Co-Publications, 8 Bradbury Street, London N16 8JN

Acknowledgements

This book has been produced as part of the LCT London Co-operative Training Programme, with finacial assistance from the London Boroughs Grants Scheme.

The publishers gratefully acknowledge the permission of the Registrar of Companies and the Registrar of Friendly Societies to reproduce the forms used in this book

Funded by

LONDON
BOROUGHS
GRANTS
SCHEME

British Library Cataloguing in Publication Data

Cockerton, Peter
  A handbook for secretaries of co-operatives
  1.Cooperative societies — Great Britain
  2.Secretaries — Great Britain
  3.Office practice — Handbooks, manuals,
  etc.
  I. Title
  334   *HD3485.A4*

  ISBN 0-946776-12-1

Cover design Helen Kozich
Printed by Calvert's Press (Workers' Co-operative)
31/39 Redchurch Street, London E2 7DJ

Preface

Ever since the first version of the Industrial Common Ownership Movement's (ICOM's) Model Rules for Workers' Co-operatives were made available in 1976, I've been aware of the need for an easy-to-understand book to enable people in co-operatives to carry out the function of secretary of the co-op. To the uninitiated the problems of dealing with the legal red tape and completing the necessary forms can be quite daunting. This book has been written to solve those difficulties.

I would like to acknowledge the help and support given by many people whilst I was writing this book. In particular I would like to thank Malcolm Lynch, Alice Holt, Charlie Cattell, Rosemary Bell and Marion Barnett for commenting on early versions of the text. I am especially grateful to Malcolm for his help with the sections dealing with contracts and equal opportunities. My thanks are also due to Tony Booth, my colleagues at Cambridge Co-operative Development Agency and Delta-T Devices, and to my family, for their support and encouragement. Finally I would like to thank Paul Rutishauser of ICOM Co-Publications for guiding me through the many problems that have arisen to a successful conclusion.

I hope that you will find this book easy to read and simple to use. If you have any suggestions for ways in which you would like to see it improved, please write to me via the publishers and I will consider incorporating your suggestions into future editions.

Peter Cockerton
Cambridge
1 May 1988.

The forms reproduced in this book are generally available free of charge or for a nominal fee from the appropriate registrar or ICOM.

Whilst every care has been taken in compiling this handbook, the author and publisher do not hold themselves responsible for any errors or omissions.

Contents

Section 1

Introduction

This book is designed to help members of workers co-operatives understand their legal and statutory obligations. It is mainly to help the secretary of the co-operative to fulfil their function of keeping the members informed and making sure that the co-operative complies with the various pieces of red tape. The secretary is required to complete many forms to keep the co-operative going legally and many examples of these forms appear in this book with notes on how to complete them.

What is written is not meant to be a definitive statement of the law. In most cases what you will need to do in a particular instance will be staightforward and obvious, but if you are in any doubt about the legal implications of what you are doing get advice. Talk to your local Co-operative Development Agency (CDA), the Industrial Common Ownership Movement (ICOM) or contact a lawyer.

Many of the concepts used in the book may be a little foreign to the philosophy of your co-operative. In law one named person, for example the secretary, may be responsible for certain matters. This may not be easy to reconcile with ideas of joint and equal responsibility by the members of a co-operative, or with job rotation etc. The best way to look at this may be to say that all the members of a co-operative are responsible for making sure that all the tasks which need to be done are carried out, and that the person appointed as secretary is supported by all the members of the co-operative in that role.

The book is divided into sections which correspond to the life of a co-operative. In this first section, there is an overview of the law, a discussion of who will use this book, and comments about the several different model constitutions for workers co-operatives and their differences.

The second section covers the matters to be dealt with immediately on starting-up the co-operative: the duties and responsibilities of the members, the management committee, the secretary and treasurer; the issuing of membership certificates; making the first entries in the co-operative's official registers (the statutory books); organizing meetings.

The third section looks at the other legal matters which usually, but not always, need to be dealt with in the first year of the life of a co-operative, but which don't often need to be dealt with at the time of start-up. Examples of these are the annual general meeting, producing accounts, appointing auditors, and dealing with contracts and debentures.

The fourth section deals with the things to do when making changes in the personnel or structure of the co-operative. For example what should happen when members come and go and how to make changes in the management committee.

The final section deals with some of the issues and matters to do in the case of a co-operative getting into financial difficulties or dying. It is hoped that you won't in practice need to refer to these sections on winding-up, insolvency and disqualification of management committee members — but the information is there if you need it!

How to use this book

Whilst you would be advised to read through the whole of the book to familiarise yourself with the responsibilities and functions of the secretary of a co-op it is likely that at some stage you will want to refer back to it about a specific subject. In this case make use of the Contents page or Index page.

You will find that different aspects of the same subject are covered in different places in the book, and you may need to search for these separate entries to get a complete picture. For example, in the case of members of the co-operative, the first members are dealt with in section 2 as are membership certificates, however making changes in the membership are dealt with in section 4. Where something is dealt with in more detail elsewhere in the book this is indicated by the use of italics (e.g. *membership certificates*). Refer to the index to find the pages where more information can be obtained. Similarly where an organization or publication is mentioned, an entry in bold (e.g. **ICOM**) indicates further details can be found in the information section at the end of the book.

Do you need to be a legal expert?

Not at all. This book is designed for people with little or no knowledge of legal matters. In each section things that you can do yourself are described in simple terms and guidance is given on when to seek further advice from **ICOM**, your local **CDA** or a lawyer.

What sort of organizations does the book cover?

Although this book is designed mainly to assist people in common ownership workers co-operatives using ICOM model constitutions much of it is relevant to other organizations.

Much of the material for *co-operative societies* applies to any society registered under the Industrial & Provident Societies Acts.

Much of the material for *co-operative companies* will apply to companies limited by guarantee without a share capital. For example many voluntary organizations use this form of legal structure.

Organizations which do not have model workers co-operative constitutions should be prepared to refer to their rules to discover where these differ from those described in the text.

Terminology used

It is necessary to distinguish between the two types of co-operative: those registered as companies and those registered as industrial & provident societies. In this book the first type are referred to as *co-operative companies* and the second type as *co-operative societies*.

Different types of model constitution for workers co-operatives use different titles to refer to the co-operative's management committee. For example in the ICOM company co-operative (or *'blue rules co-operative'*) constitution it is called the 'general council' and in the Leicester model company co-operative (or *'yellow rules' co-operative*) it is called the 'workers collective'. In this book the expression *management committee* is used to describe all such committees, including those where all members of the co-operative are also members of its management committee.

The law

Co-operatives are governed by two classes of law depending on their constitution and registration. *Co-operative societies* are governed by the Industrial & Provident Societies Acts 1965-78 and administered by the **Registrar of Friendly Societies**. *Co-operative companies* are governed by the Companies Act 1985 and administered by the **Registrar of Companies**.

The Industrial and Provident Societies (I&PS) Acts are much simpler and shorter than the Companies Act and a number of matters dealt with in the Companies Act do not appear in the I&PS Acts. When this is the case it is usually safest to assume that company law applies to co-operative societies in relation to these specific matters.

The other substantial piece of legislation which covers both societies and companies is the Insolvency Act 1986. This covers many of the matters dealt with in section 5 concerning the winding-up of co-operatives.

This book is written to comply with the law in England and Wales and legal references are up to date as at the time of publication. The law for co-operatives in Scotland and Northern Ireland is very similar to the law in England and Wales and most of this book is applicable there also. Co-operatives in Scotland and Northern Ireland should check with their legal advisers if in any doubt about specific legal issues being applicable.

The constitution

All co-operatives have a constitution which is a set of legal rules known as either *the rules* in co-operative societies or *the memorandum & articles of association* in co-operative companies. The co-operative's constitution and the relevant laws govern the way in which the co-operative will operate.

Generally the constitution will not need to be referred to often but the secretary should know and understand it should any questions or disputes arise about the legal organization of the co-operative. Each member of the co-operative should be given a copy of the constitution; a copy should be kept readily available for reference.

Main elements of the constitution

Most workers co-operatives are incorporated using model constitutions drawn up by **ICOM**. The main elements of such a constitution are as follows:
- the co-operative's official *name*
- the *trading objects* for which the co-operative has been set up, for example, "the production, distribution, hire and sale of film and video recordings"
- a *social objects* clause is usually included which demonstrates that the co-operative is interested in wider issues than simply trading:

   > "In carrying out the aforesaid objects the co-operative shall have regard to promoting the physical, mental and spiritual well-being of the community and especially those who participate in the activities of the co-operative by reason of employment in or purchasing from or selling to the co-operative and to assist people in need by any means whatsoever."
   > (from the ICOM *'white rules'* co-operative society constitution)

- powers: the co-operative gives itself the legal powers to carry out its objectives
- *shares*: each member has a £1 nominal value share. In co-operative companies, there are no shares, each member guarantees to pay £1 in the event of the co-operative going into liquidation
- membership: only employees can be *members* of a workers co-operative (with the exception of founder members, who need not be employees). The co-operative may define the word 'employee' as it wishes — it can include

unpaid volunteer employees if necessary. Any such definition should be agreed upon and written down to avoid disputes about membership eligibility

- restrictions on borrowing: for historical reasons co-operatives are barred by their constitutions from borrowing money from private sources at unacceptably high rates of interest.
- management of the co-operative and the *management committee*: this section of the constitution deals with how many members are on the committee, how they are appointed, how often it meets etc.
- *general meetings*: how often and how they are organized and the *quorum* — the number of members that have to be present to make the meeting legally valid — normally 50% of the membership
- *voting*: it is a co-operative principle that each member has one vote in meetings. Usually voting has to be by members present in person — proxy voting, where a member may be allowed to vote on behalf of another who is absent, is normally not allowed.
- the *secretary* and *treasurer*: how they are appointed and removed from office
- the *annual general meeting*: how it is organized and the matters to be dealt with at it
- investment of funds: regulations dealing with investments
- application of profits: generally profits may be added to the co-operative's general reserve, paid as a bonus to members or used to make payments in respect of social and charitable objects (see above)
- *auditors*: how they are appointed and what they should do
- *records* and *seal*: standard regulations concerning keeping books and records and using the co-operative's seal properly
- amendments to the rules: the procedure to follow when amending the constitution
- dissolution: the procedure to follow if the co-operative is wound-up. This is the clause which defines *common ownership*, stating that the assets may not be distributed amongst the members but must be passed on to either another co-operative or to a central fund maintained for co-operatives.

The preamble, secondary rules and standing orders

In addition to the legal constitution many co-operatives have additional secondary rules. These do not have the same legal force as the constitution and they can be easily changed by the co-operative at a general meeting. (Changes to the legal constitution have to be made as laid down by the constitution, they have to comply with the law, and must be registered with the appropriate registrar.)

These secondary rules can take several forms:
- they may be a statement of aims or preamble to the constitution drawn up by the founders when the co-operative was formed
- they may be a set of secondary rules or standing orders. These may be a collection of important policy and operational decisions made by the co-operative over the years. Often it is a good idea to collate these decisions together with an index so that they are readily accessible and may be referred to from time to time

Challenges to the way the co-operative is organized

Generally speaking it is up to each co-operative to interpret its own constitution. If necessary **ICOM**, a local **CDA** or a lawyer can offer advice and assist in the understanding of these matters.

Examples of circumstances where a legal interpretation might be needed are:
- where the co-operative is concerned that its activities may not entirely be covered by its *objects clauses*. In this case the co-operative may be acting outside of its powers or *ultra vires* in legal terminology (for more information see section 4)
- where an *auditor* raises a question about the co-operative's activities which needs a legal opinion
- where a member of the co-operative disagrees with the way in which the co-operative is being run and believes that rules are being broken.

In this last case if the member is unable to resolve the differences with the co-operative then the member may seek legal advice or indeed in an extreme case take the co-operative to court. It should be noted that in the case of co-operatives using the *yellow rules* constitution that there is provision for an arbitrator to be appointed to sort out disputes of this type.

Summary of differences between ICOM Model constitutions for workers co-operatives:

	White Rules	Blue Rules	Yellow Rules
society or company?	society	company	company
registered under	Industrial & Provident Societies Acts	Companies Act	Companies Act
rules or memorandum & articles?	rules	memorandum & articles	memorandum & articles
shares or guarantees?	shares	guarantees	guarantees
minimum no of members	7	2	2
name of management committee	management committee	general council	workers collective
number of committee members	5 - 19	2 - 20	2 - 25
elected at	AGM	AGM	all co-op members on committee
general meetings:	regular	quarterly	annual
notice	7 days	14 days	21 days
secretary appointed by	general meeting	general council	workers collective
treasurer appointed by	general meeting	no treasurer in constitution	no treasurer in constitution
restricted borrowing clause?	yes	no	yes
decisions made by	majority voting	majority voting	consensus
automatic membership of co-operative by employees?	no	no	yes

Note: This table is meant to detail only the main differences between the types of model constitution.

Section 2

Starting the Co-operative

In this section it is assumed that the co-operative has been registered and is about to commence business. The necessary papers have been sent to the appropriate Registrar and a Certificate of Incorporation *co-operative company* or Registration Certificate *co-operative society* has been received. The secretary should ensure that the co-operative has kept a copy of all the papers sent for registration.

Because of the assumption that the co-op has already been formed, a number of matters which are normally considered when a co-op is being set up are ommitted from this section. Examples are: the *name* of the co-op, the address of its *registered office*, and the number of members registered. Information about these items can be found in section 4 - Making Changes. The *constitutions* of co-ops were discussed in section 1.

For co-ops registering through ICOM, these are the documents they will have received after registration:

Co-op companies:

- six copies of their *memorandum and articles* of association; one company *register*
- one *common seal*
- one *certificate of incorporation*
- one blank Form 224 concerning the co-op's *accounting reference date*.

Co-op societies:

- one set of original rules with the Registrar's certificate on the back
- one *common seal*.

Now is the time to go through the formalities concerning the legal nature of the co-op: issuing *membership certificates* to the members, starting to fill in the official *registers* for the co-op, informing the members of the *management committee* of their duties and responsibilities. These are some of the items dealt with in detail in this section.

Initial membership of the co-operative

The first members of the co-operative will be those people who signed the papers sent to the Registrar for registration. Now that the co-op has been registered it is necessary formally to issue membership certificates.

Sample membership certificates for co-operative societies and co-operative companies are printed on page 12. For co-operative societies the membership certificates are share certificates; for co-operative companies the certificates are called certificates of mutual security. The co-operative may purchase certificates from ICOM or print or type its own. Certificates should be consecutively numbered.

It should be noted that co-op companies do not legally need to issue certificates of mutual security, but it is good practice to do so.

Membership certificates are usually issued under the *seal* of the co-operative.

The steps to be gone through are as follows:

Co-operative society

Call a *general meeting* of the co-operative. Record in the minutes that, "the seal of the co-operative was applied to membership certificates nos. _ _ _ _ to _ _ _ _". Seal the certificates and sign them. The secretary of the co-operative should issue them to the members in exchange for a payment of £1.
Ensure that all initial members have a copy of the rules of the co-op. Details of the certificates should be entered in the co-operative's *register*.

Co-operative company

Call a *management committee* meeting. Record in the *minutes* that "the seal of the co-operative was applied to membership certificates nos. _ _ _ _ to _ _ _ _". Seal the certificates and sign them. The secretary of the co-operative should then issue them to the members in exchange for which the members should sign the company's *register*. Ensure that all initial members have a copy of the *memorandum and articles* of the company.

The management committee

All co-ops have a two-tier decision making structure: the *general meeting* which consists of all members, and an elected *management committee*. Legally all workers' co-operatives are run and managed by their management committee. However, in many small co-ops, particularly at start-up, all the members of the co-op are members of the committee. In this case where only some of the members are to become the initial members of the management committee it is likely to have been decided at or prior to the time of registration.

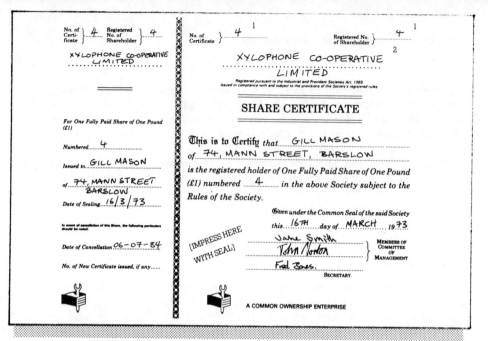

Share Certificate (Membership Certificate) — Co-operative Society
(source:ICOM)

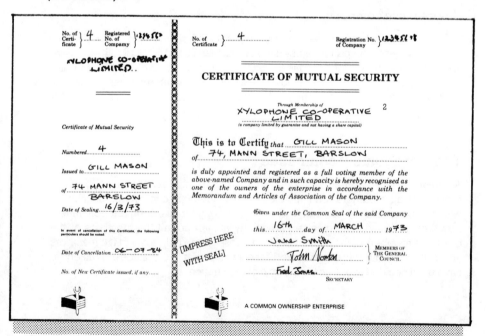

Certificate of Mutual Security (Membership Certificate) — Co-operative Company — *(source: ICOM)*

1 Not necessarily the same numbers   2 Full name of Co-op

Registration of initial committee members

Co-operative society

The names of the initial members of the management committee should be agreed by the whole membership in a general meeting. If all members of the co-op are automatically to be members of the management committee, a statement to this effect should be agreed and minuted at the first general meeting of the co-op. The names of the management committee members should be recorded in the co-operative's *register* and each member should either sign a statement saying, "I consent to being a member of the management committee", or sign the register.

Ensure that all members of the management committee have a copy of the *rules* of the co-operative. The names of management committee members are not registered with the **Registrar of Friendly Societies** except at the time of the *annual return*.

Co-operative company

The members of the management committee are technically the directors of a co-operative company. The initial committee members are usually decided prior to incorporation by all the members and the management committee members would have signed a statement of consent as part of the documents sent to the Registrar. Ensure that each member of the management committee has a copy of the *memorandum and articles* of the company. The secretary should ensure that the co-operative has a copy of all the papers sent for registration including the particulars of the first directors and their consents to act. (Form 10 sent to the Registrar of Companies is a 'statement of first directors and secretary and intended situation of registered office'. It contains details of the first directors and secretary and they each sign it to the effect that they consent to act as director or secretary of the company.)

If, for the time being, all future members of the co-op are automatically to become members of the management committee, a statement to this effect should be agreed and minuted at the first *general meeting* of the co-op.

First secretary

The first secretary will be the person who has been chosen by the initial members of the co-operative as secretary to sign the papers sent for registration.

First treasurer

A co-operative does not legally need to appoint a treasurer or finance officer but most do so. Treasurers are specifically mentioned in the constitutions of co-operative societies but not usually in co-operative companies. Many co-ops will have decided who will be the first treasurer at the time of registration. However if this has not been done the procedure for appointment should be as follows:

Co-operative society

The treasurer is appointed by a *general meeting*. The appointment should be recorded in the minutes of the meeting and noted in the co-operative's register. The treasurer need not be a member of the co-op's management committee but in most cases is likely to be a member of it.

Co-operative company

As the appointment of the treasurer is not usually mentioned in the constitution, it is up to the co-operative to decide whether it wishes to have a treasurer and how a treasurer is to be appointed and removed — whether by the general meeting or by the management committee

These decisions would normally be taken by a general meeting of the co-op. A treasurer would not be a member of the co-op's management committee unless elected to it.

Duties and responsibilities of the secretary

The secretary is usually responsible for all the legal aspects involved in running a co-operative business. Unless another person is given overall responsibility in legal matters then it is the secretary's responsibility. The following paragraphs are a basic summary of the various aspects of this work. Many of these matters are dealt with in more detail later in the book:

- dealing with official communications: certain documents (e.g. from the auditor or from the Registrar of Companies) are addressed to the secretary and it is the secretary's responsibility to ensure that these matters are dealt with promptly and effectively. Ensure that a system exists which routes all such papers to the secretary.
- overseeing all the legal aspects of that co-operative's operations. Is the co-op operating within the law? What laws in particular apply to the co-op? Examples are Employment Law and Health and Safety at Work; Factories Act; Offices, Shops and Railway Premises Act. If you are unsure about this

you can contact your local **Co-operative Development Agency, ICOM** or other advisory bodies. Through these find out about getting training. Also it is useful to subscribe to an updated digest on the subject such as **Croner's Employment Law.** Other sources of help and information include relevant government departments — such as the **Department of Employment's Small Firms Service.**

- being responsible for the proper organization of *meetings.* Again, in the absence of particular arrangements making others responsible, it is the secretary's duty to ensure that meetings are properly organized. Agendas need to be agreed, minutes (or a record of decisions) noted and circulated, notices of the meeting should be sent out to members or posted on a notice board as necessary. Even if someone else is actually responsible the secretary should ensure that the methods and systems used are appropriate and in order.

- maintaining the *statutory records* of the co-op and ensuring that the appropriate forms are filed with the Registrar. Forms have to be filed with the Registrar to deal with most *changes* in the organization of the co-op, examples are: management committee changes (companies only); name changes; registered office address changes. Blank forms can be obtained free of charge from both Registrars. It is vital that a copy is kept of all correspondence with the Registrar and of all forms sent in for filing. These copies then can form a chronological file which mirrors the file which is available from the Registrar for public inspection. The auditor will also want to see this file to check that the necessary forms have been filed correctly.

- in the absence of a clear chain of responsibility the secretary is responsible for *contracts* entered into by the co-op such as hire purchase agreements, leases, distribution agreements. In particular, the secretary has responsibility for contracts which are concerned with property. The secretary should ensure that important contracts are kept in a safe place and can be referred to easily.

- the secretary is responsible for custody of the co-operative's *seal* and ensuring that it is only used with the appropriate authority.

- in the absence of a specific person delegated to the role, it is the secretary's responsibility to ensure that the correct procedures about admitting *new members* are followed, that all members, both new and old, are kept informed of their duties and responsibilities. Management committee members and other officials such as the treasurer should also be informed of their duties and responsibilities.

- the secretary is responsible for ensuring that full and correct information about the co-operative is given on *stationery,* to comply with the law. The secretary should also ensure that the co-operative's name is clearly displayed outside the *registered office.*

- the secretary is responsible for the completion of the *annual return* form which is sent to the Registrar. This would normally be done in conjunction with the treasurer and the auditor.

- in many co-ops the secretary is responsible for seeing that the co-op has proper *insurance*. Legally the co-op only needs employer's liability insurance, but most co-ops are fully insured with a complete insurance package dealing with the co-op's premises etc.

- the secretary should ensure that each member (but not volunteer member) and employee of the co-operative has an *employment contract*. ICOM have available a **Model Employment Contract for Workers Co-operatives** which is designed especially for co-ops and is simple to adapt for your own use.

How skilled need the secretary be?

In a small co-operative the secretary need not have specialist legal skills, but instead should have a degree of common sense and good organizational skills. But it is obviously essential that the person knows their own limitations and where to get advice when they need it. A secretary without legal skill, who is acting in a reasonable manner, is not expected in law to know what a fully trained lawyer would know. A lot of the queries will be complicated so don't expect to know all the answers and don't be afraid of asking advice either from specialist agencies or, occasionally, seek the services of a lawyer. Examples of when the latter would be necessary would be:

- to check a complicated lease or other legal document
- to check or draft a specialized or important (expensive) contract or agreement
- to advise in a dispute
- to check employment rights

Try to select a lawyer who is sympathetic to co-op ideas and ideals, ask your local Co-operative Development Agency for advice in choosing one or try to get a personal recommendation. Ask for an estimate of the lawyer's fee when you outline the problem.

Duties of the treasurer

The treasurer's duties are not defined in law, but they should be defined by the co-op. What follows are a number of the duties and responsibilities that might be appropriate for a co-op treasurer and you can add to them or alter them if you wish.

The treasurer should have overall responsibility for all the financial transactions of the co-op and should ensure that proper systems for dealing with finance are in place. They should make sure that full and correct records are kept and that the bookkeeping systems are adequate. They should produce regular financial information, such as interim accounts, to facilitate the running of the co-op. The treasurer should liaise with the *auditor* and provide them with the draft of the *annual accounts*.

Obviously the extent to which a co-op treasurer can do these things will depend on their level of competence. It is important that people don't get out of their depth and that the operation of the systems and information required are within the capabilities of the people involved. Regular contact with the auditor is important to ensure that the systems are up to the standard required.

In some co-ops the treasurer will also be the bookkeeper. It is better practice, if the co-op is large enough, to have different people doing these two jobs.

The treasurer is responsible for the arrangements with the bank as to who will sign cheques etc. For a full discussion of this see the section on *bank mandates*.

Duties of management committee members

In law the members of the *management committee* of a co-operative are treated as being exactly equivalent to the directors of a limited company.

The day-to-day running of a co-operative is controlled by its management committee. Generally the management committee is given power by the general meeting (the entire membership) to exercise all the legal powers of the co-operative. The management committee members are responsible to the general meeting for ensuring that the co-operative properly carries out its business. An individual management committee member can enter into a contract on behalf of the co-operative, but the co-op may wish to limit this power by, for example, passing a resolution at a general meeting insisting that all contracts are entered into by two members of the committee.

In many small co-ops, particularly in the early stages, all members of the co-op may automatically be members of its management committee. In this case members may overlook the seriousness of their responsibilities in law and it is the secretary's job to ensure that they are aware of the facts.

The broad code of practice that management committee members should follow is:
- to exercise their powers for the benefit of the co-op and its members — not themselves
- to avoid conflicts of interest: if a matter arises at a management committee meeting in which a member has a personal interest they must declare it and not vote on the issue. There are exceptions to this rule however, the most

general one being that most constitutions allow management committee members not to declare an interest in matters connected with their own contracts of employment

- the co-op's affairs must be kept confidential: both matters about the co-op's business generally, and individual member's private details
- members of the management committee should ensure that they are obtaining sufficient and appropriate information, both from co-op members and from outside advisers, to enable them to make the necessary decisions to operate the co-operative
- they must also prevent the co-op from acting illegally or engaging in *fraudulent trading* (trading when knowingly insolvent).

Members of a co-op management committee can be held liable for the debts and liabilities of the co-op in two important cases: if they knowingly allow illegal transactions to take place or if they allow the co-op to engage in fraudulent trading — continuing to trade when they know that the co-op cannot meet its debts. If a member of a management committee is in any doubt about the financial situation of their co-op and whether it should continue trading they should seek professional advice immediately. Advice should be sought before placing any further orders with suppliers or paying any debts. Taking this action may help to prevent the committee members becoming personally liable. In the worst case a member of a management committee may be jointly and severally liable with the other members for the debts and liabilities of the co-op. This effectively means that any member can be sued for any amount to cover the co-op's debts and in practice those members with most wealth will be sued first. Further, a member may in this process be made bankrupt and as a consequence may not be allowed to be a director of a company (or management committee member of a co-op) for five years. For more information see section 5.

A director is expected to show levels of skill, care and competence appropriate to their actual knowledge and experience. A person with a higher level of expertise, for example, a qualified accountant, would be expected to demonstrate a correspondingly greater degree of competence. Members of management committees are unlikely to be penalised if they acted reasonably within the scope of their owns skills and experience even if technical offences have been committed. For a complete list of such offences see schedule 24 of the **Companies Act 1985**.

Personal liability

The circumstances where a management committee member can lose their limited liability and become personally liable to the co-op are:

- if you were negligent and did not act with due skill and care in making a decision, for example by not taking notice of a financial forecast

- if you failed to act because of ignorance in a situation where you should have been aware of the facts. For example if you continued to make financial decisions without ensuring that you were receiving the appropriate reports and therefore having no way of knowing whether your decisions were the right ones to make or if you were aware that the co-operative was acting illegally but took no action to deal with the problem.

You can become personally liable as a management committee member, not only to your co-operative, but to third parties as well:

- if the co-operative acts outside of its powers (known as ultra vires in law). This might happen if a co-operative does something which its objects do not give it the power to do although most co-operatives using ICOM model constitutions have wide enough powers to do most things. If in doubt, especially if your co-operative wishes to trade in a type of business not specifically mentioned in its objects, you should seek advice
- if your co-operative gets into a situation where it is engaged in fraudulent trading as above.

Under certain circumstances you may be individually liable to third parties. Usually management committee members may be reimbursed by their co-op for any cost incurred on behalf of the co-op but there are exceptions to be aware of:

- if you entered a contract on behalf of the co-op without having obtained the necessary approval to do so
- if you entered into a contract giving the impression that it is a personal one when it is intended to be a contract between the third party and your co-op
- if you sign a contract in a personal way instead of signing it 'for and on behalf of XYZ Co-op Limited'.
- if you inititate or become involved in a deliberate, illegal act, for example a fraud.

Statutory books (registers)

It is a legal requirement that all registered co-ops (companies or societies) keep a set of records concerning the membership of the co-op and its management committee. These records should be readily available for any member who wishes to see them.

It is the secretary's legal responsibility to ensure that the records are kept up-to-date and the secretary can be fined for not doing so. Lists of the records for co-operative societies and companies are as follows.

The standard list for a *co-operative company* is:

- Register of members
- Register of directors (members of *management committee*)
- Register of secretaries

○ Register of treasurers (optional)
● Copy of *annual returns*
● Register of charges (mortgages/debentures)
● Register of *debenture* holders
○ List of *certificates of mutual security* (membership certificates) (optional)
● Minute book(s) for *general meetings* and *management committee meetings* (may be separate)
● Sealing register (list of documents issued bearing *common seal*).

Standard books are available, both bound and loose leaf, for these registers and they are straightforward to fill in. **ICOM** has produced a standard register especially for co-operative companies limited by guarantee. Other examples are available from law stationers, but as these will usually be drawn up with share capital companies in mind they generally need small adaptations for use by co-operative companies.

The standard list of records required for a *co-operative society* is:
● Register of members
● Register of *management committee* members
● Register of secretaries
● Register of treasurers
● Copy of *annual returns*
● Register of charges (mortgages/debentures)
● Register of share certificates (*membership certificates*)
● Minute book(s) of *general meetings* and *management committee meetings* (may be separate)
● Sealing register (list of documents issued bearing *common seal*)

At the time of writing standard books are not available for co-operative societies and so I set out the details of each Register on pages 21–22. ICOM is currently producing a register for co-operative societies which should be available shortly.

It is sensible to keep a photocopy of the annual return together with a copy of the audited accounts in a file. This can be the same file that you use to keep copies of all official correspondence, copies of forms etc. sent to the Registrar of Friendly Societies.

Register of members

Member ref no.	full name	address	date of becoming member	date of ceasing to be member	share cert. no.[1]	sec's initials
1	FRED JONES	12 ARCADIA AVENUE BAR	12·09·72	06·07·84	1	FJ
2	JANE SMITH	25 MAIN ST, BARSLOW	12·09·72		2	FJ
3	JOHN NORTON	63, LONG RD, CLEEBAR	12·09·72		3	FJ
4	GILL MASON	74, MANN ST. BARSLOW	16·03·73	06·07·84	4	FJ

[and so on (minimum 7 members)]

1 Note: this is the number taken from the *share certificate register* (see below). It is not necessarily the same number as the member's reference number.

Register of management committee members, secretaries, treasurers

The format of these registers is similar. Three separate registers should be drawn up following this example:

Secty[1] ref no.	full name	address	date of becoming secretary	date of ceasing to be sec.	mem ref no.[2]	signature confirming entry[3]
1	FRED JONES	12 ARCADIA AVENUE, BARSLOW	12.09.72	05.04.80	1	F.Jones.
2	GILL MASON	74 MANN STREET, BARSLOW	05.04.80	14.02.82	4	G.Mason
3	JANE SMITH	25 MAIN STREET, BARSLOW	14.02.82		2	Jane Smith

[etc.]

Notes: 1 or treasurer or management committee member

2 entered from *register of members* (see above)

3 members sign to show that they accept responsibility for the post where all members of the co-op are automatically members of the management committee, this fact should be noted in the register of management committee members.

Register of charges (including mortgages and debentures)

This register is used to record all *charges*, *mortgages* and *debentures* issued by the co-operative (usually as security for loans). Draw one up following this example:

ref no	date of charge	short description of charge	value if appropriate	names and addresses of persons entitled to the charge	date of complete or partial[1] satisfaction	amount paid off
1	12.12.83	A debenture being a fixed and floating charge on all the co-op property and undertaking both present and future	£3000	Cambridge CDA Ltd [etc.]		

1 'Date of complete or partial satisfaction' is to show the date when, for example, the loan has been paid off and the debenture cancelled (see *debentures*, cancellation.)

Register of shares (membership certificates)

share no.	full name and address of holder	date of issue	date and amount of payment	mem.'s ref no.[1]	secretary's initials	date of Member leaving & forfeiting share
1	JANE SMITH, 25 MAIN STREET, BARSLOW.	12.09.72	12.09.72 : £1	2	F.J.	
2	FRED JONES, 12 ARCADIA AVENUE BARSLOW.	12.09.72	12.09.72 : £1	1	F.J.	06.07.84
3	JOHN NORTON, 63 LONG ROAD, CLEEBAR	12.09.72	12.09.72 : £1	3	F.J.	
4	GILL MASON, 74 MANN ... BARSLOW	16.03.73	16.03.73 : £1	4	F.J.	06.07.84

1 This is the number taken from the *register of members* (see above).

The common seal

Every registered co-operative, whether a *co-operative company* or a *co-operative society*, must by law have a common seal. A seal comprises two metal discs which when squeezed together in a letter press make an impression showing the co-op's name on a piece of paper sandwiched between the two discs.

Seals may be obtained direct from **ICOM** or a law stationers and cost about £15.00. If by any chance your co-op hasn't got one, obtain one immediately because you will be unable to complete certain transactions, such as leases, without it.

The seal is used as the co-op's official legal 'signature' on the following documents:
- conveyances, leases and other legal documents
- share and loan certificates

A self-adhesive red disc is normally fixed to the paper before being sealed and the seal is pressed in the centre of the red disc. You can obtain a supply of these discs, also called 'seals', from a law stationers, but usually the solicitor preparing a document requiring a seal, such as a lease, will supply one. Your own share certificates don't need the red seal to validate them legally, just the common seal's impression.

The seal may only be used on the authority of the appropriate meeting or committee of the co-operative as defined by the *rules* or *memorandum and articles*. A list should be kept of all documents sealed as well as a note made in the minutes of the appropriate meeting.

Stationery requirements

To comply with the law the following information needs to be written on letterheads and other stationery and applies to both co-op companies and co-op societies:
- the co-op's name. You may also have a trading name for business purposes in addition to this name (e.g. 'Triangle Wholefoods Collective Limited trading as Suma Wholefoods').
- the address of the *registered office* must be given. If more than one address is shown the registered office address must be identified.
- one of the following narrations:

    'Registered in England and Wales'

    'Registered in Wales'   for companies

or

    'Registered in England'

    'Registered in Scotland'

'Registered in Northern Ireland' for societies

- the number given to your co-op by the appropriate Registrar: e.g. 'Registered No.: 123456 (R) — societies are identified by the suffix 'R'.

The following are optional additions to this list:
  o the VAT number
  o the narration 'A Workers Co-operative' or something similar
  o names of management committee members or co-op members. The rule here is you must list all members of the management committee or co-op, or none. In such a list you must state the nationalities of any non-EEC nationals. Since the membership of a co-op's management committee may be subject to regular changes, it is cheaper not to print the names of the committee members.

The stationery which needs this information includes: letter paper, letterheads, catalogues, price lists, order forms and other official documents and publications. Cheques and other official bank documents, official publications and invoices must show the full name of the co-op company or society.

Use of abbreviations

It is important that you quote the name of your co-operative in exactly the same form as its registered name to remain within the law. For example if your co-op's name is 'Cambridge Bakery Co-operative Limited', you should ensure that this is not shortened to 'CBC Ltd.' on letterheads etc. This does not stop you from referring to CBC as long as you include the correct, full name somewhere on the item of stationery.

The word 'Limited' and the abbreviation 'Ltd.' are not interchangeable. Companies may use either form when registering but societies must not use the abbreviated form. Always use the form with which the co-operative was registered on all your stationery.

Most co-ops will have printed letterheads but many do not need to go to the expense of printing invoices and similar forms. In these cases it is useful to get a rubber stamp (or a supply of small sticky labels) with the necessary information.

Standard letterheads can be obtained from **ICOM**.

**A stamp suitable for
official use on invoices
etc.**

XYZ CO-OP LIMITED
12 CHURCH STREET
WOLVERHAMPTON
W6 9QL   (Reg. Office)
PHONE 0486 - 789101
Reg. in England No 12345R   VAT No: 123-4567-89

Display of name

It is a legal requirement that all co-ops, companies and societies, must exhibit their full name on the outside of every office or other place where their business is carried out. The name must be legible and in a conspicuous position. For example, if you work from offices it can be on the door to your office or on the main notice board of the office block.

Display of documents at registered office

It is a legal requirement that the following documents are prominently displayed at each co-op's *registered office*:

- *certificate of incorporation* (co-operative companies only) and any further certificates relating to change of name etc. In the case of co-op societies the Registrar of Friendly Societies does not issue a certificate of incorporation, but instead attaches a sealed 'acknowledgement of registration' to a copy of the registered rules. This should be kept safely by the co-op secretary but not necessarily displayed. If you lose your certificate a duplicate can be obtained from the appropriate registrar
- certificate of employer's liability insurance. Check with your insurance broker about this, or if you have not got a broker ask your local **Co-operative Development Agency** or **ICOM** for advice.

- a notice of ownership of any business names used. Just a simple notice will suffice for this saying that your business name is owned by the co-operative.

You may also display:
- o a VAT certificate if applicable. Display is optional, not a legal requirement, although you must register for VAT if your turnover is greater than £22,100. (limit as at March 1988).

Meetings

Meetings are at the centre of the life of the co-operative so it is vitally important to make sure that they happen in the best and most effective way.

This section deals with two sorts of meetings: *general meetings* and *management committee* meetings. In co-operatives where all the members are also members of the management committee the distinction between the two sorts of meetings may be blurred and it is therefore of importance for the secretary to grasp the essentials of the differences between the two. When disputes occur it is important to be clear as to which meetings made which decisions.

General meetings

General meetings are meetings of all the members of a co-operative. The rules for calling and conducting general meetings are laid down in the constitution of the co-operative. There are three types of general meeting.
- *ordinary general meetings* (OGMs) are regular, planned general meetings — often held by co-operatives for the whole membership to hear reports from and question the management committee.
- *extraordinary general meetings* (EGMs) are special meetings called for a specific purpose for example to change the constitution of a co-operative.
- the *annual general meeting* (AGM) is the general meeting held annually to consider the annual report and accounts and elect the management committee.

Notices

The following periods of notice should be given for general meetings:

	Co-operative societies	Co-operative Companies
OGMs	7 days	14 days or 21 days if a *special resolution* is to be presented
EGMs	7 days	14 days or 21 days if a *special resolution* is to be presented

Notices must be displayed in a conspicuous place that all members know about, or sent by post through the internal mail or individually to members at their homes. In the case of co-op companies where a special resolution is to be put, the notices must be given individually to the members or sent by post to their private addresses. Notices must list the purpose of the meeting and contain an agenda.

Notices of all general meetings must also be sent to the auditors of the co-op and to any debenture holders. (This applies to co-operative companies only.)

Procedure at general meetings

At the start of each meeting a chair is elected whose job is to conduct the meeting in an orderly manner. However it is perfectly possible for the co-operative to agree that the same person will act as chair of general meetings for a period of time, for example a year.

It is good practice, but not a legal requirement, to make decisions at general meetings by passing resolutions. This means that for a matter to be discussed a member must propose a resolution such as, "This co-operative will adopt an equal opportunities policy". The resolution should then be seconded by another member. Amendments to the resolution can be proposed by other members and accepted or rejected by the meeting. The amended resolution is then debated and put to the vote. If passed by a simple majority the resolution is carried and becomes policy of the co-operative.

It is useful to extract these important policy decisions and place them in a special book. In time they become the 'secondary rules' of the co-op.

Many co-ops operate more informal arrangements than these, and there is no objection to this practice, as long as the decision making procedures are seen to work well. The method of running meetings is often written down as part of the *secondary rules* or *standing orders* — the by-laws of the co-op.

Resolutions in writing

Exceptionally, it may be appropriate to ask **all** the members to sign their names to a resolution rather than call a meeting. In this case the resolution has the same force as one duly passed at a general meeting. Obviously this procedure can only be used in small co-operatives and should the matter prove to be controversial then a meeting should be called to discuss it.

The *quorum* at general meetings — the number of members required to be present for the meeting to be valid — is usually fifty per cent of the membership of the co-operative. You should check your *constitution* on this point if you're not using model rules. The meeting should not be allowed to commence unless a quorum is present.

In the event of a quorum not being present at a company co-op general meeting the meeting may be adjourned to the same place and time one week later. At such an adjourned meeting only the business which was on the original agenda may be discussed. At the adjourned meeting if a quorum is not present within half an hour of the start of the meeting then the members present constitute a quorum.

No procedure is written in the model rules of co-op societies to deal with the situation of a quorum not being present. It is suggested that in this case the meeting be adjourned and strenuous efforts made to ensure that a quorum is present at the adjourned meeting. If desired, procedures for dealing with the lack of a quorum can be dealt with in a co-operative society's secondary rules.

Voting at general meetings is usually by members present in person. Proxy voting, where a person is given the power to vote for another not actually present, is usually not allowed. Each member has one vote. Voting is normally taken by a show of hands but a poll may be demanded. In this case there may be either a secret ballot or a public ballot. In a secret ballot members should cast their votes on slips of paper which are then counted by two 'tellers' agreed by the members. In a public ballot each member's vote is recorded in the *minutes* of the meeting.

Resolutions are decided by simple majority vote except for *special resolutions* which must be passed by a three-quarters majority of members present in person. (An example of a special resolution is a resolution seeking changes in the co-op's constitution, further information about this is given in section 4.)

However if a co-operative wishes informally to operate a consensus method of decision making it may do so. But any such informal arrangement may be challenged by a member drawing attention to the co-operative's constitution.

A consensus method of decision making involves the members discussing the issues concerned for as long as is necessary until all agree on the matter to be decided. If consensus cannot be achieved then the proposal is lost. This method usually works better in small groups than in larger ones where it can give rise to people using the procedures unscrupulously to 'veto' decisions that they disagree with.

Management committee meetings

The management committee needs to meet frequently and regularly to control the day-to-day operation of the co-operative. In many co-operatives the committee meets weekly and generally it will meet at least monthly. The management committee decides how often to meet.

Notices for management committee meetings need not be posted to members of the committee but may be displayed on a notice board if preferred. It is good practice for co-ops to be flexible enough to be able to accept items up to the last minute.

Decisions at management committee meetings are made by simple majority voting (except in the case of *'yellow rules'* co-operative companies where a consensus method is used). Again, if a co-operative wishes informally to operate a consensus method of making decisions it may do so. But any such informal arrangements may be challenged by a member drawing attention to the co-operative's constitution.

Any resolution about which the management committee cannot agree — where there is a fifty-fifty voting split — is not carried unless, unusually, the constitution specifically gives the chair a second or 'casting' vote. However the resolution can be referred to a *general meeting* of the co-operative if appropriate.

A special meeting of the committee can be requested to be held at any reasonable time by any one member of the management committee. It is up the the members to define 'reasonable'.

Each meeting of the management committee can elect one of their members to chair the meeting. But, again, this does not prevent the committee agreeing that the same person will be the chair of the committee for a period (e.g. a year) if this helps the functioning of the committee.

Instead of having a committee meeting, all the members of a management committee may sign a written resolution which then has the same effect as a resolution duly passed at a management committee meeting. This procedure can be used to pass non-contentious emergency resolutions when action is needed immediately.

Minutes of general meetings

The secretary should ensure that minutes, full and correct records of proceedings, are kept at general meetings. The minutes should include as a minimum:
* the date, time and place of the meeting
* a list of those present, or if that number is large, over 30, an estimation of the number of members present
* a note of who was in the chair — especially if different from meeting to meeting
* a note of apologies for absence
* a list of resolutions with the names of those proposing and seconding them as well as a note of whether or not the resolution was carried
* a summary of the debate on each resolution
* a note of any other decision agreed by the meeting

The minutes can if desired be a much fuller record of the proceedings than this minimum suggestion.

Copies of the minutes should be circulated to the members or kept in a place where members can have access to them as appropriate.

Minutes of committee and sub-committee meetings

The minutes of management committee meetings should comprise a record of the decisions made at each meeting. If the meetings tend to be formal then a record such as that suggested for general meetings is appropriate.

Alternatively a much simpler method is to record the decisions made by the meeting and the names of those present in a 'Decision Book' or 'Minute Book' which is written up at the time of the meeting itself and is kept in place where committee members can refer to it.

It may be necessary to distinguish between those people who have the right to vote — management committee members — and those who do not have that right — other members of the co-operative. The normal practice is to refer to the former as 'present' and to the latter as 'in attendance'.

Sub-committees and working parties

The general meeting or management committee of the co-operative may set up sub-committees and working parties to deal with specific matters.

Sub-committees are generally formal and have specific long-term objectives. An example might be the marketing sub-committee which would deal with the co-op's marketing strategy and present reports on this to the management committee.

Working parties are generally informal and are often dealing with short-term matters. An example might be a 'new-person working party' responsible for drawing up an advertisement and job description for a new member of the co-op and then presenting these items to the management committee for approval.

Each working party and sub-committee should be given precise terms of reference. The membership of the groups should be decided by the meeting that sets up the group up. Minutes should be kept in the same manner as for management committee meetings.

Bank mandates

The question of the commercial relationship of the co-op with its bank is not one dealt with in this book. From the secretary's point of view the important considerations are the question of the bank mandate and making ·changes to cheque signatories — those people who can sign cheques. In a co-op this matter can present problems if the co-op has a high turnover of members and if it is thought appropriate that a larger number of members have the power to sign cheques.

The conventional wisdom on the matter of cheque signatories is that it is essential to have cheques signed by two people rather than by just one in order to safeguard against theft.

The safest and most controllable system is one where the treasurer keeps the cheque book and signs all the cheques as they are needed which are then countersigned by one out of two specifically authorized members of the management committee of the co-op. This ensures that the treasurer can maintain full control over expenditure.

However, in many co-ops it is the practice for many members of the management committee, or even all, to have the power to sign cheques but with two people having to sign each cheque. The disadvantage of this system is that it may allow poor control of current expenditure and, for example, not enable the level of a bank overdraft to be kept at a minimum. It may also make for difficulties in keeping records of expenditure. The co-op's auditors may also consider this to be bad practice.

Other co-ops may allow a single signature on cheques up to a certain amount , say £100, and require two signatures on cheques with a higher value. The problem with this method is essentially one of enforcement. Who will ensure that the system is not abused, can a bank be relied on to throw out a cheque for £105 with only one signature on it? Such a system will work effectively only if there is good internal control and discipline. It is definitely not recommended.

Each bank has its own mandate forms and these are different for co-operative societies and companies. Printed on pages 35–36 are the relevant sections of the Co-op Bank's mandate. Completing it is straightforward but make sure you keep a copy for your files. The bank will require a copy of your constitution, and if you are borrowing, regular copies of your accounts. Any changes to the bank mandate, such as change of bank, or change of signatories to the account, should be recorded in the minutes of the appropriate management committee or general meeting.

It may be simpler to make a completely new mandate with the bank than alter an old one, as alterations can lead to a very confused situation over time, and it may be difficult for both the bank and the co-op to be clear as to who is, in fact, an authorized signatory.

It is essential that the co-op is operating its bank account with a correct mandate and that the full name of the co-op, including the word 'limited', appears on cheques and other documents. Where a co-op has been operating as an unincorporated association — partnership — prior to incorporation as a registered company or society it is sometimes found that the bank has not been properly notified of the change in status, and in this case the members are not protected by corporate status.

The appointment of auditors

By law every registered co-operative (society or company) must have its accounts audited by a properly qualified accountant who is practising as an auditor. The auditor cannot be an employee or member of the co-op.

To be properly qualified the auditor must be a member of one of the following bodies:

- the Institute of Chartered Accountants in England and Wales (in which case the auditor will be either ACA or FCA).
- the Institute of Chartered Accountants of Scotland (ACA, FCA).
- the Institute of Chartered Accountants of Ireland (ACA, FCA)
- the Chartered Association of Certified Accountants (FCCA, ACCA).

The only exception to this requirement for an auditor is when a co-op has been dormant and not traded throughout its financial year. It is essential to ensure that your co-operative engages a properly qualified auditor at an early stage in its life. If you use the services of an accountant who is not properly qualified, you will still need a properly qualified person to audit the accounts.

Your local **Co-operative Development Agency** may be able to advise on suitable accountants and auditors. You can check the credentials of an auditor by looking in the lists of qualified accountants in a reference library.

An auditor must be properly appointed and the appointment is usually renewed at the *AGM*. The first appointment is normally made by the *management committee* (co-operative company) or a general meeting (co-operative societies).

You should ensure that your auditor has a copy of the co-op's constitution.

Casual vacancies such as when an auditor resigns are filled by the same method as when they are initially appointed. As is explained in section 4, creditors and others may be wary of a change in auditor for no apparent reason. So change only when you have good reason to do so.

The audit requirements of co-operative companies and co-operative societies are different. Also the time limits in which various reports have to be filed differ. Further information about these are given in the next section.

The duties of the auditors are to make a report to the members of the co-op about the following matters:
- whether proper accounting records have been kept
- whether the Balance Sheet and Profit & Loss Account are in agreement with those records and express a "true and fair view" of the financial affairs of the co-operative over the period of the accounts and at the balance sheet date.

The auditors have a right of access to all the co-op's books, records and vouchers and may ask the officers of the co-op any questions that they may consider necessary to complete the audit. They also have to consider the *directors report* (company only) and check that it is consistent with the *accounts*.

If they are dissatisfied they will put a note to that effect in the report. Such a qualified auditor's report may be damaging to the co-op and restrict its ability to borrow or obtain credit. For this reason it is very important to establish a good relationship with the auditor and ensure in particular that all the accounting systems meet with the auditor's approval.

Remuneration of auditors may be decided by an *AGM* or left to the co-operative's management committee as appropriate.

Application for an account

1   Full name by which the account is to be known   XYLOPHONE CO-OPERATIVE LIMITED

2   Nature of business or organisation   DISTRIBUTION OF MUSICAL RECORDINGS

3   Address (including postcode) of registered office, business, partnership or organisation   17 MILL END, BARSLOW

   Telephone number of business or organisation   (0742) 666332

4   Name and address (including postcode) to which all communications are to be sent   AS 3.

5   Type of current account you require   Current ☑   Cheque & Interest ☐

   Type of deposit account you require   7 days notice of withdrawal ☑   One month's notice of withdrawal ☐   Top Tier (three months notice) ☐

6   Name of Co-operative Society and Handybank at which you would like to make deposits and/or cash cheques   BUXTON CO-OPERATIVE SOCIETY   BARSLOW BRANCH

   Limit you request for cashing cheques   £ 500   per month

7   Name and address of present bankers   NONE

8   Name and address of previous bankers   NONE

- **Sole traders** — please now complete **question 9 only.**
- **Partnerships** — please now complete **question 10 only.**
- **Limited companies** — please now complete [2] **questions 11 and 14 only.**

- **Societies** registered under the Industrial and Provident Societies Acts — please now complete **questions 12 and 14 only.**
- **Organisations** (trade unions, friendly societies, clubs and societies not registered under the Acts) — please now complete **questions 13 and 14 only.**

11   Limited companies

*either [2]

Signature of the person completing questions 1-8   Fred Jones.   Date   12/9/72

Position in the company   SECRETARY

Please send with the completed form:
- an up-to-date and true copy of the Memorandum and Articles of Association;
- the Certificate of Incorporation;
- if yours is a public company, the 'Trading Certificate' entitling the company to start business.

Please now complete **question 14**

1 co-op societies

2 co-op companies

Bank Mandate — *(source: Co-op Bank) continued over page*

12 Societies registered under the Industrial and Provident Societies Act

Signature of the person completing questions 1-8   *Fred Jones.*   Date   12/9/72   *or

Position in the Society   SECRETARY

Please send with the completed form a true copy of the rules, certified as being up-to-date. Please now complete **question 14.**

---

14 Certified copy of resolutions

made by the limited company, society or organisation

The following resolutions were passed at a meeting of the Directors/Committee* held on

Date   12 / 9 / 7 2

It was resolved that:

a   The Co-operative Bank p.l.c. ('the Bank') shall be appointed our bankers;

b   The Bank shall be authorised to honour all cheques or other orders for payment drawn, made or accepted on our behalf including bills of exchange and promissory notes, even if any such payment causes any accounts to be overdrawn or increase any existing overdraft, provided that such documents are signed by:

any one of the signatories ☐   any two of them ☑

both of them ☐   all of them ☐
or enter the correct details here

in accordance with the specimen signatures;

c   The Bank shall act on all specimen signatures in accordance with any instruction, notice, request or other document in writing concerning our account (including the opening of new accounts), affairs or property;

d   The Bank shall be sent a copy of any future resolutions which affect the terms of the above resolutions;

e   The Bank shall be sent a copy of any changes in our Rules/Memorandum and Articles of Association/Regulations or Bye-laws*;

f   The Bank shall be notified in writing of any change of Directors/Committee members*;   2

g   The Bank shall be notified in writing of any change of officials authorised to sign on our behalf.

It is certified that these resolutions have been recorded in the Minute Book and signed by the Chairman and that the specimen signatures shown overleaf are correct.

Date   12 / 9 / 7 2

Chairman's signature

Secretary's signature   *Fred Jones.*

* Delete as appropriate

Name	Description of status (director, secretary, chairman, treasurer, committee member)	Signature
JANE SMITH	CO-OP MEMBER	*Jane Smith*
FRED JONES	SECRETARY	*Fred Jones.*
JOHN NORTON	CO-OP MEMBER	*John Norton*
GILL MASON	CO-OP MEMBER	*Gill Mason*

1   co-op societies

2   Directors for co-op companies, committee for co-op society

Section 3

Running the co-operative

This section deals with many of the matters that have to be dealt with by the secretary of a co-operative after it has started-up. Many of the items need to be dealt with regularly, for example the accounts and the annual general meeting; the other items occur only occasionally.

The section deals with the following matters:
- the annual general meeting
- extraordinary general meetings
- accounts
- directors' report (management committee report)
- annual returns
- contracts
- debentures and charges
- other legal requirements
- equal opportunities

The annual general meeting

Traditionally the purpose of the *annual general meeting* (AGM) of an organization is for the management to present a report and accounts and to answer questions from the whole membership.

This is formally the purpose of an AGM for a co-operative but obviously the actual nature of the AGM will depend a great deal on whether the co-op is large or small. For example, in a small co-op the AGM may take two minutes at the end of a management committee meeting. But even so all the formalities of sending out notices etc. must still be gone through.

The essential elements of the AGM and the matters leading up to it are as follows:
- the accounts and draft management committee report are prepared and sent to the *auditor* (co-operative companies only)
- the auditor sends the audited accounts and report to the management committee for approval
- the management committee agrees a date for the AGM and an *agenda*
- notices of the AGM are circulated to the members, the auditor and the debenture holders, if any, of the co-op 21 days prior to the AGM. The notices include:
    the agenda
    a copy of the approved and audited accounts and report
    information about voting at the AGM and nominations for the management committee.

A specimen agenda and nomination paper are printed on page 39.

**Specimen
agenda**

The first AGM of XYZ Co-op Limited will be held on 8th June 1988 at 2.30 p.m. at 75 High Street, Bridgeton.

Agenda:

1. Apologies for Absence
2. Minutes of Previous AGM [if any]
3. To receive the accounts for the year ended 31.03.88 together with the management committee's report
4. To elect the management committee
5. To reappoint the auditors Messrs Mills and Co. at a fee to be agreed by the management committee.

Nomination papers for membership of the management committee are enclosed.

I _ _ _ _ _ _ _ _ _ _, a member of XYZ Co-op Limited, hereby nominate

_ _ _ _ _ _ _ _ _ _, a member of XYZ Co-op Limited to be a member of the co-operative's management committee.
[or Secretary or Treasurer of the co-operative, as appropriate]

Signed: _ _ _ _ _ _ _ _ _ _
Seconded by: _ _ _ _ _ _ _ _ _ _
[also a member of the co-op]
"I consent to being nominated for this position"
Signed: _ _ _ _ _ _ _ _ _ _
Date: /   /   19

Specimen nomination paper

At the AGM the procedure is as follows:
- members are identified and asked to sign the attendance register
- the meeting is conducted by the chair in accordance with the agenda
- elections are held for the management committee
- minutes are kept by the secretary or by someone else and then checked by the secretary.

After the AGM

The secretary completes the *annual return* in the case of a co-op company or, in the case of a co-operative society, this is done by the auditor. In either case it is up to the secretary to see that it is done. For a company co-op the annual return must be filed within 42 days of the AGM.

Extraordinary general meetings

Extraordinary general meetings (EGMs) are usually called when there is special and important business for the co-operative to consider. An example would be a proposed change in the co-op's *constitution*. An EGM can be called by the management committee or by one tenth of the membership of the co-operative. The purpose of the meeting must be stated. If the members request that an EGM be called, it is up to the management committee to convene it. If they fail to do so within twenty one days of being asked the members may convene the EGM themselves within three months of the original asking date.

Accounts and financial year ends

Every co-operative must keep a full set of accounting records and produce, at least, annual accounts which can be presented to the members and placed on the public record.

It is good practice to appoint an auditor at the earliest possible date and to discuss with that person the co-op's accounting requirements and bookkeeping system. It is vital to ensure you tell the auditor at an early stage whether you are a co-operative company or co-operative society and to give them a copy of your constitution.

The requirements for companies to keep accounts are set out in the **Companies Act 1985**. The format of the accounts is specified in Schedule 4 of the Act. It is the job of the co-op's treasurer in conjunction with its auditor to ensure that the co-op's accounts meet these requirements. The profit and loss accounts must give a true and fair view of the profit or loss of the business for the financial year and the balance sheet must give a true and fair view of the state of affairs of the business at the end of the financial year.

Other matters specified in this part of the Act include accounting rules and all the matters that need to be disclosed in the accounts.

Directors' report (management committee report)

An essential part of the accounts — for a co-operative company only — is the directors' report. This is a written report by the directors (management committee) of the company to the members. The report must represent a fair review of the development of the business of the company during the financial year and the position at the end of the year. It must include the following details:

- names of directors (the members of management committee) during the year
- a note of the principal activities of the company (and any significant change in activities)
- significant changes in fixed assets
- a note of directors' interest in the company (not generally applicable to co-ops)
- details of political and charitable gifts made by the co-op where the amounts are greater than £200
- particulars of any significant important events in the year. It should also give an indication of significant future developments as well as indicating any significant activities in the field of research and development
- where the company has more than 250 employees:
  details of the employment of disabled people (with reference to the quota system)
  details of employee information and consultation arrangements

The directors' report will usually be drawn up by the co-op's treasurer in consultation with the management committee and the auditor.

A co-operative may wish to expand this report but it should remember that it is a public document, forming part of the accounts. A better, and more confidential method, would be to prepare a fuller annual report for limited circulation to members of the co-op and other interested parties.

If you want to use your accounts for publicity purposes you can add a chair's report to them. This can be generally glowing about the business.

G

COMPANIES FORM No. 224

Notice of accounting reference date (to be delivered within 6 months of incorporation)

224

Pursuant to section 224 of the Companies Act 1985

To the Registrar of Companies

For official use	Company number
	1 2 3 4 5 6 7 8

Name of company

* XYLOPHONE CO-OPERATIVE LIMITED

gives notice that the date on which the company's accounting reference period is to be treated as coming to an end in each successive year is as shown below:

Day   Month

3 1   1 2

5 April
Day   Month

0 5   0 4

30 June
Day   Month

3 0   0 6

31 December
Day   Month

3 1   1 2

Signed Fred Jones.   [Director][Secretary]† Date 12/9/72

Presenter's name address and reference (if any):

THE SECRETARY
XYLOPHONE
CO-OPERATIVE LIMITED

For official Use	
General Section	Post room

Form 224 — Accounting Reference Date — Co-operative company
(source: Registrar of Companies)

Accounting reference dates

Co-operative company

Every company has the opportunity to advise the Registrar of Companies within six months of incorporation of the date to which its accounts will be made up. This is called its accounting reference date (ARD). Form 224 is used for this purpose (see copy on page 42).

If the company fails to record an ARD the Registrar will regard the company's ARD as being 31st March. Before filing Form 224 you are advised to discuss with the co-op's auditor the most satisfactory ARD for your co-op.

ARDs can be changed using form 225(1). However the accounting period cannot be lengthened to more than a year more frequently than every 5 years.

Co-operative society

The Registrar of Friendly Societies requires that all societies registered under the Industrial and Provident Societies Acts will end the financial year (at the end of any month) during the period 31st August to 31st January inclusive. The date generally used is 31st December. To have a year end at any other time in the year it is necessary for the secretary to write to the Registrar to obtain a special dispensation. This is normally not difficult to obtain as long as there are good reasons for the request. Examples of valid reasons are:
- o in the case of a conversion from an existing business that the new business should have the same accounting date as the old business
- o in the case of a co-operative linked in some way with a local authority a request to use the standard local authority accounting year end, the 31st March, could be made.

The Registrar makes no charge for considering and approving a change of date and no forms are involved, the request being made by letter.

Annual returns

Co-operative company

Every company, trading or not, must make an annual return made up to any date, up to 42 days after the date of the annual general meeting (AGM) in each year.

The return must be filed with the Registrar of Companies within 42 days of the AGM. If no AGM is held a return should be sent made up to the 31st December. The appropriate return form is No: 363 and a specimen is printed on pages 44–45,

A

COMPANIES FORM No. 363

Annual return
of a company

Pursuant to sections 363 and 364 of the Companies Act 1985

363

Note The appropriate fee should accompany this form

Please do not write in this margin

To the Registrar of Companies

For official use | Company number

1 2 3 4 5 6 7 8 9

Please complete legibly, preferably in black type, or bold block lettering

Annual return of (note 1)

* **XYLOPHONE CO-OPERATIVE LIMITED**

* insert full name of company

† if the company has a share capital, this date must be the 14th day after the annual general meeting

The information in this return is as at

16 MARCH 19**88** †.(**The date of this return** note 1)

Address of registered office of the company

17 HILL END, BARSLOW | Postcode

Total amount of indebtedness of the company in respect of mortgages and charges (note 2).

£ **NIL**

If different from the registered office, state address where the register of members or any register of debenture holders or any duplicate or part of any register of debentures is kept or may be inspected.

Register of members

Register of debenture holders

Particulars of the secretary

Name (notes 3 and 4) **JANE BELL**

Previous name(s)(note 3) **SMITH**

Address (notes 4 and 5) **25 MAIN STREET BARSLOW** | Postcode **BS16 6TJ**

‡ only pages 1 and 2 need be completed in the case of a company without share capital

We certify this return which comprises pages 1, 2, [3, 4, 5 and 6]‡ [plus§ _____ continuation sheets]

§ enter number of continuation sheets attached

Signed **John Norton** Director, and **Jane Bell** Secretary

Presentor's name address and reference (if any):

For official Use
General Section | Post room

Page 1

Form 363 — Annual Return — Co-operative company
(source: Registrar of Companies)

Notes   1. dates of birth need not be given

2. where you are asked for the business

occupation of directors you may put 'member of co-op'

Notes

1. An annual return is required for every calendar year. If the company has a share capital the date of this return must be the 14th day after the date of the annual general meeting. If it does not have a share capital the date of this return must be a date not more than 42 days after the annual general meeting.

4. Where all the partners in a firm are joint secretaries, only the firm name and its principal office need be given.

   Where the secretary or one of the joint secretaries is a Scottish firm, give only the firm name and its principal office.

2. * This section should include only indebtedness in respect of charges (whenever created) of any description set out in section 396(1) of the Companies Act 1985 (in the case of English and Welsh companies) or section 410(4) of that Act (in the case of Scottish companies).

5. Usual residential address must be given. In the case of a corporation, give the registered or principal office.

6. Director includes any person who occupies the position of a director, by whatever name called, and any person in accordance with whose directions or instructions the directors of the company are accustomed to act.

3. For an individual, his present christian name(s) and surname must be given, together with any previous christian name(s) or surname(s).

   "Christian name" includes a forename. In the case of a peer or person usually known by a title different from his surname, "surname" means that title. In the case of a corporation, its corporate name must be given.

   A previous christian name or surname need not be given if.—

   (a) in the case of a married woman, it was a name by which she was known before her marriage, or

   (b) it was changed or ceased to be used at least 20 years ago, or before the person who previously used it reached the age of 18; or

   (c) in the case of a peer or a person usually known by a name by which he was known before he adopted the title or succeeded to it

7. If the space provided for listing directors is inadequate, a prescribed continuation sheet must be used.

8. The names must be given of all bodies corporate incorporated in Great Britain of which the director is also a director, or has been a director at any time during the preceding five years.

   However a present or past directorship need not be disclosed if it is, or was then been, held in a body corporate which, throughout that directorship, has been:—

   (a) a dormant company (which is a company which has had no transactions required to be entered in the company's accounting records, except any which may have arisen from the taking of shares in the company by a subscriber to the memorandum as such);

   (b) a body corporate of which the company making the return was a wholly-owned subsidiary;

   (c) a wholly-owned subsidiary of the company making the return; or

   (d) a wholly-owned subsidiary of a body corporate of which the company making the return was also a wholly owned subsidiary

9. Dates of birth need only be given if the company making the return is:—

   (a) a public company;

   (b) the subsidiary of a public company; or

   (c) the subsidiary of a public company registered in Northern Ireland

10. Include payments on application and allotment, and any sums received or shares forfeited.

11. Show all the persons currently holding shares or stock in the company at the date of the return, giving their names and addresses, the number of shares or amount of stock and details of all transfers since the last return or, if this is the first annual return of the company, all transfers since the company was incorporated. If more than one class of share is held please add more columns as appropriate.

    Additionally, show all persons and their relevant details if they have ceased to be members since the last return was made or, if this is the first return, since the company was incorporated.

If the list of members is not in alphabetical order, an index which will enable any member to be readily located within the list must be attached to this return if the space provided for listing members is inadequate, a prescribed continuation sheet is available.

If full details have been given on the return for either of the last two years, a company may, if it so wishes, or include in this section details relating to persons who since the date of the last return:

(a) have become members;

(b) have ceased to be members; or

(c) are existing members whose holdings of stock or shares have changed.

If full details have been given on the return for either of the last two years and there have been no changes please state "No Change".

12. For consistency, it is suggested that particulars should be placed opposite the name of the transferor and not opposite that of the transferee, but the name of the transferee may be inserted in the remarks column opposite the particulars of each transfer.

Particulars of the director(s) of the company (notes 6 and 7)

[1]

Name (note 3): JOHN NORTON	Business Occupation: MEMBER OF CO-OP
Previous name(s) (note 3): NONE	Nationality: BRITISH
Address (note 5): 63 LONG ROAD, CLEEBAR Postcode: BS16 7TZ	Date of birth (note 9): N/A
Other relevant past or present directorships* (note 8): NONE	

[2]

Name (note 3): GWEN STANLEY	Business Occupation: MEMBER OF CO-OP
Previous name(s) (note 3): NONE	Nationality: U.S.A.
Address (note 5): 75 STATION ROAD, BARSLOW Postcode: BS16 4TZ	Date of birth (note 9): N/A
Other relevant past or present directorships* (note 8): NONE	

[3]

Name (note 3): ANNE MILLER	Business Occupation: MEMBER OF CO-OP
Previous name(s) (note 3): NONE	Nationality: BRITISH
Address (note 5): THE BEECHES, STATION ROAD, BARSLOW Postcode: BS16 5T2	Date of birth (note 9): N/A
Other relevant past or present directorships* (note 8): BUXTON CO-OPERATIVE SOCIETY	

Name (note 3): WILLIAM STORR	Business Occupation: MEMBER OF CO-OP
Previous name(s) (note 3): NONE	Nationality: BRITISH
Address (note 5): 28, LONG DRIVE, BARSLOW Postcode: BS17 3GA	Date of birth (note 9): N/A
Other relevant past or present directorships* (note 8): TRIANGLE CO-OPERATIVE LIMITED	

Please do not write in this margin

Please complete legibly, preferably in black type, or bold blocklettering

* delete if inappropriate. Enter particulars of other director-ships held or previously held. If this space is insufficient use a continuation sheet

2P 54 1809 6 85

3. present and past directorships: mention any held in the past 5 years (even if you have stopped being a director of the organization concerned); note that membership of management committee of co-op society counts as a directorship.

forms are available free of charge from the Registrar. Only pages 1 and 2 need be completed. The current filing fee is £20. Keep a copy of the completed annual return for your own records.

It is the responsibility of the secretary to ensure that the annual return is completed and sent in. However it may be preferred that the auditor do it instead, in which case you should ensure that you are given a copy for the co-operative's files.

Co-operative society

The Registrar of Friendly Societies issues a number of different forms for the use of societies when making annual returns. An example of a form is printed on pages 47–48. The main part of the form, pages 4–11, is concerned with the accounts of the co-operative and page 12 is an auditor's report. It is suggested that the co-operative requests that its *auditor* completes the annual return as part of the audit. The auditor may prefer to attach a copy of the co-op's accounts to the form rather than complete each page — that decision is up to the auditor.

The first page of the return contains a list of the management committee. In cases where all members of the co-operative are members of the committee it is not essential to name all members of the co-op but instead to make a statement to the effect that: "all members of the co-operative are members of the management committee" ("by virtue of rule_ _ _" if it is part of the co-op's constitution). The name of the secretary must be stated. If there is no fixed chair cross out the word 'chairman'.

The annual return must be sent to the Registrar within three months of the end of the financial year. Make sure that you keep a copy of the Annual Return.

Contracts

A contract is an agreement between two parties which involves some 'consideration' given by one party to the other in exchange for a benefit given by the second party to the first. A contract may be verbal or written. The 'consideration' may be money but it does not have to be.

A co-operative may enter into a contract with another party, such a contract in writing needs to be signed by a director (a member of the management committee) unless by law the contract is required to be sealed.

A person may enter into dealings with any director of a company in good faith without making further enquiries. Any director may thus bind a co-operative by

FORM AR15
Industrial and Provident
Societies Acts 1965 to 1978

ANNUAL RETURN FOR
MISCELLANEOUS BUSINESSES

Register No. 123456'R

See notes and instructions for completion on pages 2 and 3

Year ended...... 31ST DECEMBER 19 87

Name of Society ...... XYLOPHONE CO-OPERATIVE LIMITED ......Limited

Registered Office ...... 17 HILL END, BARSLOW ...... Postcode......

Particulars of committee of management at the date 5/4/1988 on which the return is signed:

Names (block capitals)	Addresses (block capitals)	Year of birth	Business occupation and other directorships *(excluding directorships of parent or subsidiary organisation (s)).*
Chairman			
JOHN NORTON	63 LONG ROAD, CLEEBAR	1962	MEMBER OF CO-OP
GWEN STANLEY	75 STATION ROAD, BARSLOW	1965	" "
ANNE MILLER	THE BEECHES, STATION RD BARSLOW	1967	" "
WILLIAM STORR	28 LONG DRIVE, BARSLOW	1960	" "
WENDY STATHAM	16, STATION RD, BARSLOW	1964	" "
ARTHUR CURRING	12, THE STREET, CLEEBAR	1958	" "

JANE BELL Secretary	25 MAIN ST, BARSLOW	1963	MEMBER OF CO-OP

The address to which Rules, Returns and other Documents should be sent is as follows:—
ENGLAND AND WALES: Registry of Friendly Societies, 15-17 Great Marlborough Street, London W1V 2AX
SCOTLAND Registry of Friendly Societies, 58 Frederick Street, Edinburgh EH2 1NB

1

A

Notes and Instructions for completion

1 This return must be made up to a date not earlier than 31 August nor later than 31 January and sent to the Registrar not later than 31 March. A society authorised by the Registrar to make up its annual return to a date not within this period must send this return to the Registrar within three months of that date.

2 *It should be accompanied by*

(i) A copy of the auditors report (the space provided on page 12 may be used for this purpose).

(ii) A copy of each balance sheet made during the period included in the return and any report of the auditor thereon.

(iii) Where the society has a subsidiary a copy of its group accounts unless exempted from this requirement.

(iv) A copy of any current cost accounts produced in accordance with Statement of Standard Accounting Practice No. 16

3 If there is insufficient space in any part of the printed form particulars may be entered on supplementary sheets of paper of similar size to the annual return which should be attached to the return and suitably cross referenced.

2

B

The accounts contained in the annual return should comply with the following requirements:

General

1 When preparing the accounts and annual return consideration must be given to Statements of Standard Accounting Practice. Attention is also drawn to Auditing Standards and Guidelines with particular reference to the Auditor's Operational Standard and to the Guidelines headed "Accounting Systems" and "Internal Controls".

2 The accounting policies adopted by the society in determining the amounts to be included in respect of items shown in the balance sheet and in determining the income and expenditure for the year shall be stated on page 11.

3 There shall, if it is not otherwise shown, be stated by way of note to the accounts.

(i) every material respect in which items shown therein are affected:
(a) by transactions of a sort not usually undertaken by the society or otherwise of an exceptional or non-recurrent nature; or
(b) by any change in the basis of accounting

(ii) any special circumstances which affect liability in respect of taxation of profits, income or capital gains for the financial year or for succeeding financial years.

4 Any negative value to be entered shall be clearly indicated by placing the entry in brackets.

Form AR15 — Annual Return — Co-operative Society
(source: Registrar of Friendly Societies) continued over page

Section C Employees' emoluments (excluding pension scheme contributions)

Scale of successive integral multiples of £5,000 (insert appropriate steps as necessary) £	Number of employees
30,000 — 35,000	NONE
35,001 — 40,000	NONE

Number of persons employed by the society (other than committee members) whose several emoluments exceed £30,000 and fall within each step of the stated scale.

10 LOANS TO COMMITTEE MEMBERS, SECRETARY, CHIEF EXECUTIVE OFFICER AND DEPUTY CHIEF EXECUTIVE OFFICER (and to any person who after the making of a loan became a Committee member, Secretary, etc.)

	No of loans	Total amount £
1 Loans made during the period covered by the annual return		
Members of committee		
Others	NONE	
2 Loans outstanding at date of balance sheet (including loans made in previous years)		
Members of committee		
Others	NONE	

The responsibilities of the committee in relation to the accounts are defined in the Industrial and Provident Societies Act 1965 to 1978. Prior to approving the accounts the committee must satisfy itself that the Act and the requirements set out in the annual return have been complied with. In particular, if in the opinion of the committee any of the current assets do not have a value on realisation in the ordinary course of the society's business at least equal to the amount at which they stand in the accounts, that fact must be disclosed

At the meeting on 25 MARCH 1986 the accounts and balance sheet contained in this annual return were approved by the committee of management.
At the meeting on 5 th APRIL 1988 the annual return for the period ended 31st Dec. 1987 was approved by the committee of management and the undermentioned were authorised to sign it.

Signatures of

Secretary ... *Jane Bill*

Member of committee ... *G Stanley*

Member of committee ... *John Norton*

AUDITOR'S REPORT
(see guidance notes on page 3)   AS PAGE 1 OF THE ACCOUNTS

Signature(s)
Profession or calling(s) CHARTERED ACCOUNTANTS
Address(es) BLOGGS AND CO,
LEANDER HOUSE, STATION RD, BUXTON Date 25 MARCH 1988

Printed for Her Majesty's Stationery Office by Roberdene Ltd. Amersham
12 86 C5 Dd 239905

12   £1.90 net (exclusive of tax) ISBN 0 11 600418 5

C
Auditor's Report
1 The relevant statutory provisions are contained in the Industrial and Provident Societies Act 1965, Section 9(1)(a) and the Friendly and Industrial and Provident Societies Act 1968, Section 9 and Section 11
2 The report must be a report on the accounts for the period included in the return insofar as the accounts relate to that period. The report should be framed with regard to approved auditing standards
3 The space provided on page 12 may be used by the auditor either to enter the report or, where the report is not included in the accounts, to make reference to the report
3 Both the report and any reference to the report must be signed by the auditor

MEMBERS
Number of shareholding members:

at beginning of year*	4
admitted during year	2
together	9
membership ceased during year	2
at end of year	4

*if in disagreement with previous return, explain difference

STAFF

	Full time	Part time
Number of staff employed by society at end of year	4	

---

9 COMMITTEE OF MANAGEMENT AND EMPLOYEES' EMOLUMENTS etc.
Section A Committee members' emoluments, pensions and compensation

	For services as committee members £	For other services £	Total £
1 Committee members' emoluments (including pension scheme contributions)	0	60,000	60,000
2 Committee members' or past committee members' pensions	N/A	N/A	
3 Compensation to committee members or past committee members in respect of loss of office			

Section B Further particulars of committee members' emoluments
Section B is not required to be completed if the committee members' emoluments entered against item 1 of section A do not exceed £60,000

	Scale of successive integral multiples of £5,000 (insert appropriate steps as necessary) £	Number of committee members.
1 Number of committee members whose several emoluments (excluding pensions scheme contributions) fall within each step of the stated scale.	1—5,000 / 5001—10,000	6

2 Emoluments (excluding pension scheme contributions) of the chairman, or, if more than one person has been chairman during the financial year, the several emoluments of each such person so far as is attributable to the period during which he was chairman.		£ N/A
	Total	

3 Emoluments (excluding pension scheme contributions) of the committee member (if any) whose emoluments exceed the total amount entered in item 2 of this section or, if the emoluments of each of two or more of the committee members exceed the said amount, the emoluments of him (or them in the case of equality) who had the greater, or, as the case may be, the greatest.		£ 10,000

	Number of committee members	Aggregate amount of waived emoluments £
4 Committee members' emoluments (including pension scheme contributions) the rights to receive which have been waived and which, but for the waiver, would have failed to be included in the amount entered against item 1 of section A.	N/A	N/A

This margin is not to be written on

The pages included here are the sections not normally covered in the society's accounts.

entering into a contract.

Examples of contracts include:

Contracts made by other organizations with the co-op such as:
- maintenance agreements for office equipment
- bank mandates
- insurance policies
- leases and conveyances of property

Contracts made by the co-op with other organizations:
- the co-op's standard terms and conditions of sale as printed on its invoices
- royalty agreements - where a co-op agrees to pay for an author's work in return for the co-op owning the copyright
- agency agreements - where a co-op agrees to give an agency selling rights to its products

The job of the secretary should be to ensure that:
- all contracts entered into by the co-operative are properly considered by the appropriate body, whether the *general meeting*, management committee, or a specifically authorized co-op member
- written records are kept of any relevant discussions and negotiations concerning contracts
- all contracts are written, if at all possible, and are signed by a properly authorized member of the management committee, on behalf of the co-op
- verbal contracts are avoided if at all possible — especially for financial matters. If a contract is verbal the secretary should write a letter of confirmation to the other party stating the terms of the contract
- appropriate professional advice is taken.

It is up to the co-operative to decide who will be authorized to make a contract on the co-op's behalf. For example if it is one individual then all contracts should be approved by that person only. Normally however large and expensive contracts should be considered by the co-op's management committee and a member of the committee be authorized to sign the contract on behalf of the co-op.

It is essential that a management committee member signing a contract adds the words: "signed on behalf of XYZ Co-op Limited" to their signature, otherwise they could be held personally liable for the contract.

Contracts made under seal

Certain contracts, such as leases, have to be sealed by the co-op's *common seal*. In these cases, once the management committee has agreed the contract it must officially agree to seal it (co-operative company) or call a general meeting to agree for the seal to be used (co-operative society).

Drawing up and checking contracts

In general a co-op should seek professional advice in drawing up its own contracts. For a special contract, for example a royalty agreement, it may be necessary to deal with a lawyer specializing in this sort of work. To find an adviser contact **ICOM**, your local **Co-operative Development Agency** or a lawyer.

Advice may also need to be taken when entering into a contract if it is important for the co-op's commercial existence or has large financial implications.

Contracts between the co-op, members and supporters

It is essential that a co-op draws up and executes proper written contracts between itself and its members and supporters to cover such items as:
- *employment contracts*
- loan agreements covering loans from members and supporters to the co-op (see the **ICOM Loan Finance Pack**)

Frequently these matters are overlooked, but it is only fair to all concerned that they are dealt with properly and speedily.

Debentures and charges

A co-operative needing a loan from a bank may be asked to provide the security for the loan in the form of a debenture or charge.

A debenture is a document usually issued under seal by a co-operative as security for a loan. It contains a promise to pay an amount by a certain date and almost invariably creates a charge on the whole or part of the property of the company.

The word 'charge' means approximately the same as a mortgage except that a charge is not necessarily secured on property. A debenture is a device used by a lender to arrange for some security over their loan. The effect of the debenture, by creating a charge, is to ensure that in the event of the co-operative ceasing to trade, or becoming insolvent, the debenture holder is paid in preference to unsecured creditors. Often the debenture holder has the power to appoint a receiver in the event of the co-op defaulting on payment. Common forms of debenture are:

- a fixed and floating charge on the co-operatives' undertaking and property past, present and future
- a charge on book debts of the co-operative
- a specific fixed charge on land and buildings or plant and machinery

A floating charge will be paid out after statutory preferential creditors such as VAT, PAYE etc. A specific charge on book debts or specific plant and machinery will be paid out preferentially over all other creditors.

Should a co-operative be seeking a loan, for example from a bank, it would be a good idea to investigate whether the bank could take a debenture as security for the loan. A debenture is much more preferable from the co-op's point of view to other alternatives such as personal guarantees. Using a debenture does not put any member personally at risk and maintains the equality of members. The use of personal guarantees will inevitably mean that members with more personal assets become more vulnerable than those with less — in times of trouble the banks will inevitably go for the member with the most resources first.

Form of debenture

The lender will usually provide a standard form of debenture which the co-op should approve at a management committee meeting (co-operative company) or a general meeting (co-operative society) and authorize the co-operative's seal to be affixed. Read the debenture carefully and if in doubt discuss it with your advisers.

If your co-op wishes to make a loan to another co-op and wishes to secure the loan with a debenture, suitable forms are available from **ICOM** or law stationers but advice should be obtained first.

Further information about these matters is given in the **ICOM Loan Finance Pack** which includes facts about loans to co-ops, guarantees, debentures etc. It also contains specimen forms and advice on how to complete them.

Registration of debentures

Co-operative company

A debenture issued by a co-operative company is not valid until registered by the Registrar of Companies. The debenture must be sent to the Registrar within 21 days of its creation. Usually the debenture holder will take responsibility for registration (using Form 47). However if the co-operative has to register its own debenture it is vitally important to complete the registration forms correctly otherwise the registration may fail. Get advice on this. There is no registration fee. The Registrar will issue a certificate of registration and return the debenture duly marked. The debenture should be kept by the co-op's bank in its safe and a copy kept by the co-op.

Co-operative society

There is no need for debentures issued by co-operative societies to be registered with the Registrar of Friendly Societies. But if the debenture is not registered enforcement of it will be made more difficult. If either the debenture holder or the co-op wishes to register the debenture on the public record either party may do so but a certified copy of the debenture must be sent to the Registrar of Friendly Societies within 14 days of execution together with a completed Form AI. The fee for registration is £1. The Registrar will send an acknowledgement on Form AJ.

Issuing further Debentures

It is a normal condition of debentures that once a co-operative has issued a debenture it cannot issue any more without the permission of the first debenture holder. In the event of a second debenture being issued the question of 'ranking' arises. (Unless both debentures are 'fixed charges' on different items of the co-operative's property.)

'Ranking' is the order in which each debenture will be paid, the priority of each lender. If the first lender is a bank it is likely that they will make sure that if a second debenture is issued that the second lender will have no rights to the assets of the co-op until they, the first lender, has been paid in full. It is not uncommon for a co-op to issue two debentures in this way.

The co-operative should keep a *register of debentures* as described in section 2.

Cancellation of debentures

Once the loan for which the co-op issued a debenture has been repaid in full the debenture should be cancelled. The debenture holder will return the debenture to the co-op and the co-op then needs to complete the procedure for cancellation.

Co-operative Company

- cancel the debenture by writing the word 'cancelled' across it in large letters

- complete Form 403a and take it to a solicitor or other commissioner for oaths
- send the completed Form 403a to the Registrar of Companies.

Co-operative society

- cancel the debenture by writing the word 'cancelled' across it in large letters
- complete the following stages only if the debenture was registered (see above)

    complete Form AL and take it to a solicitor or other commissioner for oaths

    send the completed Form AL to the Registrar of Friendly Societies.

Loans to members of the management committee

This applies to *co-operative companies* only. Companies are in general not allowed to make loans to directors — that is members of the management committee in a co-operative. But there are a number of exceptions to this rule:

- loans up to a total value of £2500 are exempt
- directors must have sufficient funds to carry out their work — thus advances for travel expenses etc. are acceptable.

Clearly advice should be sought if a co-op wishes to makes loans greater than £2500 to management committee members for purposes not connected with the co-op's business.

Other legal requirements

This is a short, non-exclusive summary of other legal requirements for co-operatives.

Employment Law: each employee must have a statement of the terms and conditions of their employment within 13 weeks of starting work. In addition to this it is good practice to issue the *contract of employment* within 13 weeks.

Health and safety: the co-operative should comply with health and safety legislation, the Factories Act (if applicable) the Offices, Shops and Railway Premises Act. For more information see **Croner's Reference Book for Employers**. Your local Co-operative Development Agency or library should have a copy you can refer to.

Insurance: the co-operative must have employers' liability insurance. For insurance advice contact your local Co-operative Development Agency to find the name of local insurance brokers.

Equal Opportunities Law: all employers have a duty not to discriminate on the grounds of sex and race against people who are in employment or seeking employment with them. As a co-op it would be expected that you not only observe the law, but do something positive to combat discrimination.

The secretary is responsible for ensuring that the law is complied with in the area of equal opportunities:

- it is illegal to treat a person less favourably on the grounds of race or nationality
- it is illegal to treat a person less favourably on the grounds of sexual or marital status
- under the Equal Pay Act women are generally entitled to the same terms and conditions of employment as men
- all employers with more than 20 employees have a duty to employ a quota of disabled people.

For further information see the Codes of Practice issued by the **Commission for Racial Equality**, the **Equal Opportunities Commission** and the **Manpower Services Commission** (the latter refers to the employment of disabled people). These are helpful pamphlets and should be read before taking on new employees or, conversely, considering taking disciplinary action against an employee.

The co-op may wish to draw up an equal opportunities policy in which case a model can be obtained from the Equal Opportunities Commission.

Employing disabled people

The standard quota for disabled people is 3% of the work-force — there should be at least one disabled person amongst every 33 employees. It is not however an offence to be below the quota. For co-op companies of over 250 employees the annual *management committee report* which accompanies the annual accounts must include a statement describing the co-op's policy towards disabled employees.

Grants may be available to enable co-ops to convert their premises so that they are suitable for disabled people.

Section 4

Making changes

This section deals with the things to be done by the secretary when the co-operative makes changes:
- changes in the co-op's membership
- changes in the management committee
- changes in the secretary and treasurer
- changes of the registered office address, number of members, name, constitution or objects of the co-operative
- changes of the co-op's auditors.

In most cases the procedure for dealing with changes in the co-op is quite simple and just a matter of completing the necessary paperwork. Many of the changes need official forms to be completed and sent to the appropriate Registrar. Blank forms are available free of charge from the Registrar, ICOM or your local Co-operative Development Agency. It is good practice to keep photocopies of all forms sent to the Registrar for the co-op's records. The Registrar of Companies does not normally issue acknowledgements of forms received, but if you enclose a duplicate copy of your form when sending it in for filing, the Registrar will stamp the duplicate and return it to you. This is a useful proof that your co-op's public file has been amended and is up to date.

In the unfortunate event that your co-op has not kept copies of forms filed with the Registrar you may ask for a photocopy of your public file. You will be charged for this service. Or you can inspect your file for a small fee. The **Registrar of Companies** maintains files on microfiche in Cardiff and London and you can see them on demand. In the case of the **Registrar of Friendly Societies** it is best to phone for an appointment.

Changes in membership of the co-operative

The admission of new members should be agreed at a *general meeting* of the co-operative. A *membership certificate/share certificate* (for co-operative societies) or *certificate of mutual security* (for co-operative companies) should be sealed with the co-op's *seal* at the general meeting and given to the member. In the case of a co-operative society the member should pay £1 for the share.

The new member should be issued with a copy of the *rules* of the society or *constitution* of the company as appropriate. An entry should be made by the secretary in the *register of members*.

In the case where all members of the co-op are members of the management committee see the procedure for new *management committee* members below.

When a member ceases to be a member of the co-op that fact should be noted in the minutes of a general meeting and the secretary should make appropriate entries in the register of members.

In the case of a co-operative society, where the member has a £1 share, the £1 belongs to the co-op when the member leaves.

In *common ownership* co-operatives the departing member is not entitled to any share of the assets of the co-op on departure.

There is a minimum number of members that must belong to a co-operative. For co-operative companies this number is 2 and for co-operative societies it is 7. If the membership falls below this the remaining members may become personally liable for the debts of the co-op and it may be wound up by the Registrar.

Changes in the management committee

Changes in the membership of management committees of workers co-operatives are generally made by election at an *annual general meeting* (AGM). However in some co-operatives the general meeting may elect new members of the management committee from time to time.

In the case where all members of the co-op are automatically members of the management committee, changes are agreed at a general meeting.

The secretary of the co-op should see that the following steps are completed:
* the new management committee members should be informed of their duties and responsibilities
* make the appropriate entries in the *register of management committee members* (directors) for both new and departing management committee members.
* In the case of company co-ops notify the Registrar of Companies of the changes using Form 288, which the new management committee member must sign to show that they consent to being a director. The form must be sent to the Registrar within 14 days of the change. No fee is payable. A copy of the Form is on pages 58–9.

Do not forget to inform the Registrar of any members resigning from the management committee (also using Form 288). Keep a photocopy of the form for the co-op's records.

G

Notice of change of directors or secretaries or in their particulars

288

Pursuant to section 288 of the Companies Act 1985

Please do not write in this margin

Please complete legibly, preferably in black type, or bold block lettering

* insert full name of company

o specify the change and di ereof anu .. this consists of the appointment of a new director or secretary complete the box below. If this space is insufficient use a continuation sheet.

§ Applicable to directors only

† delete as appropriate

To the Registrar of Companies

For official use

Company number
123456789

Name of company

• XYLOPHONE CO-OPERATIVE LTD

notifies you of the following change(s):

ø AT THE GENERAL MEETING ON THE 14TH MARCH 1988, GWEN STANLEY WAS ELECTED A DIRECTOR AND FRANCIS MURDOCH RESIGNED AS A DIRECTOR.

Particulars of new director or secretary (see note 1)

Name (note 2 and 3) GWEN STANLEY	Business occupation§ MEMBER OF CO-OPERATIVE	1
Previous name(s) (note 2) NONE	Nationality§ U.S.A.	
Address (notes 3 and 4) 75 STATION ROAD		
BARSLOW	Date of birth (where applicable)	2
Postcode BS16 4CZ	(note 5)§ N/A	
Other directorships (note 6)§		
NONE		

I consent to act as [director][secretary]† of the company named above

Signature **G Stanley**

Date 14/3/88

Continued overleaf

Presentor's name address and reference (if any):

THE SECRETARY
XYLOPHONE CO-OPERATIVE
LTD

For official Use

General Section | Post room

Page 1

Form 288 — Notice of Change of Directors or Secretaries — Co-operative company (source: Registrar of Companies)

Particulars of new director or secretary (see note 1) continued

Name (note 2 and 3)	Business occupation§	§ applicable to directors only.
Previous name(s) (note 2)	Nationality§	
Address (notes 3 and 4)		
Postcode	Date of birth (where applicable) (note 5)§	

Other directorships (note 6)§

I consent to act as [director] [secretary]† of the company named on page 1

Signature   Date

† delete as appropriate

number of continuation sheets attached (see note 7)

Signature *Jane Bell*   [Director][Secretary]† Date   14/3/88

Notes

1 'Director' includes any person who occupies the position of a director, by whatever name called, and any person in accordance with whose directions or instructions the directors of the company are accustomed to act.

2. For an individual, his present christian name(s) and surname must be given, together with any previous Christian name(s) or surname(s).

   "Christian name" includes a forename. In the case of a peer or person usually known by a title different from his surname, "surname" means that title. In the case of a corporation, its corporate name must be given.

   A previous christian name or surname need not be given if:—

   (a) in the case of a married woman, it was a name by which she was known before her marriage; or

   (b) it was changed or ceased to be used at least 20 years ago, or before the person who previously used it reached the age of 18; or

   (c) in the case of a peer or a person usually known by a British title different from his surname, it was a name by which he was known before he adopted the title or succeeded to it

3 Where all the partners in a firm are joint secretaries, only the firm's name and its principal office need be given.

   Where the secretary or one of the joint secretaries is a Scottish firm, give only the firm name and its principal office.

4 Usual residential address must be given. In the case of a corporation, give the registered or principal office.

5 Date of birth need only be given if the company making the return is:—

   (a) a public company;
   (b) the subsidiary of a public company; or
   (c) the subsidiary of a public company registered in Northern Ireland

6 The names must be given of all bodies corporate incorporated in Great Britain of which the director is also a director, or has been a director at any time during the preceding five years.

   However a present or past directorship need not be disclosed if it is, or has been, held in a body corporate which, throughout that directorship, has been:—

   (a) a dormant company (which is a company which has had no transactions required to be entered in the company's accounting records, except any which may have arisen from the taking of shares in the company by a subscriber to the memorandum as such).

   (b) a body corporate of which the company making the return was a wholly-owned subsidiary;

   (c) a wholly-owned subsidiary of the company making the return; or

   (d) a wholly-owned subsidiary of a body corporate of which the company making the return was also a wholly owned subsidiary.

7 If the space overleaf is insufficient, the names and particulars must be entered on the prescribed continuation sheet(s).

Page 2

1 member of co-operative is sufficient

2 dates of birth need not be given

Changes in the treasurer or secretary of the co-operative

A new treasurer or secretary of the co-operative may be appointed by the management committee or general meeting depending on the co-op's rules or constitution.

The new official should be told of their duties and responsibilities. Training courses for new officers may be available — check with your local **Co-operative Development Agency**.

Appropriate entries should be made in the *register of treasurers/ secretaries*.

In the case of company co-ops the Registrar of Companies should be notified of the change of secretary (but not treasurer) on Form 288 as above.

Change of registered office address

The Registered Office is the address to which all official communications to your co-op can be directed, for example: letters from the Registrar of Companies or Friendly Societies; legal matters (e.g. writs); letters to the secretary of the co-operative.

The address chosen is normally the address of the co-operative's office but it does not need to be a place from which the business is actually trading. There are no planning permission implications and, especially in the early stages of the business, it may be that a member's home address is the one chosen.

Changing the address of your registered office is comparatively simple. For a *co-operative company* the stages to go through are as follows:
- decide on your new registered office address (probably your new trading address). Agree this at an appropriate meeting (e.g. management committee meeting) and record it in the minute book
- complete Company Form 287 (see specimen on page 61)
- send the completed form to the Registrar of Companies within 14 days of passing the resolution. There is no fee payable. Keep a photocopy of the form for the co-op's records.

The procedure for changing the registered office address of a *co-operative* society is complicated by the fact that the address is printed in the rules, for example Rule

COMPANIES FORM No. 287

Notice of change in situation of registered office

287

Pursuant to section 287 of the Companies Act 1985

To the Registrar of Companies

For official use

Company number

| | | | | 1 2 3 4 5 6 7 8 9 |

Name of company

* XYLOPHONE CO-OPERATIVE LIMITED

gives notice that the situation of the registered office of the company has been changed to:

49 HILL END, BARSLOW

Postcode **BS 16 2LS**

Signed Jane Bell [Director][Secretary]† Date 31/3/88

Presentor's name address and reference (if any):

THE SECRETARY
XYLOPHONE CO-OPERATIVE
LIMITED.

For official Use
General Section

Post room

Form 287 — Notice of Change in Situation of Registered Office — Co-operative company *(source: Registrar of Companies)*

4 of an ICOM *'white rules'* co-op. The stages to go through are as follows:
- decide on your new registered office address (probably your new trading address). Agree this at an appropriate meeting (e.g. co-op management committee meeting) and record it in the minute book
- complete I&PS Form I (see specimen on page 63)
- send completed Form I to the Registrar of Friendly Societies immediately with the appropriate fee
- the Registrar will send an acknowledgement on Form J. You should note that the change is effective only from the time of registration
- amend your rules to give the new registered office address; destroy old copies of the rules and make new copies for distribution to members and others (e.g. your bank). Take care not to destroy your original set of rules with the Registrar's Certificate attached to it.

Changing the registered number of members

This procedure applies to a co-operative company only. The *articles of association* specify the maximum number of members of the company. In the Leicester Model *'yellow rules'* co-op this is 25; in the standard ICOM *'blue rules'* Model this number is 500. If you have any choice in the matter it is probably better to register a large number, such as 500, when you incorporate to save having to change it later.

If the number of members of your co-operative exceeds this number, then the number must be altered. It is suggested that you alter it so that the new number will be appropriate for the foreseeable future. You should use the following procedure:
- write to the **Registrar of Companies** to explain the position
- pass a resolution at a management committee meeting that the number should be changed
- notify the Registrar of the change in writing — keep a copy of the letter
- amend your articles of association to show the new number —amend any copies also.

Changing the name of the co-operative

You should exercise care when choosing a name for your co-operative, as many names are unacceptable. In particular the following questions need to be considered:
- is the name similar to one already on the Register of Company Names (or does it sound similar)? Check the copy of the register in your local reference library to verify this, or ask ICOM.

INDUSTRIAL AND PROVIDENT SOCIETIES
ACT 1965

Notice of Change in Situation of Registered Office pursuant to section 10 of the Act

Name of Society .... X Y L O P H O N E C O - O P E R A T I V E ....

.... Limited

Register No. .... 1 2 3 4 5 6 ...... R

To the Central Officer

Notice is hereby given that the above-mentioned society

on ...... 31ST MARCH ...... 19 88 ..... changed the situation

of its registered office from ... 17, HILL END, ...

.... BARSLOW .... (Postcode) ....

to ... 49 HILL END, BARSLOW ....

.... (Postcode) ... BS16 2CS

Signed on behalf of the Society

Jane Bell

....
Secretary

Date ... 31ST MARCH 1988

HMSO Bil 017614/1

Form I — Notice of Change in Situation of Registered Office — Co-operative society *(source: Registrar of Friendly Societies)*

- does the name contain any 'code words' for which special permission must be sought? Examples are:

    — words which imply national or international pre-eminence (e.g. 'National'; 'British').

    — words which imply governmental patronage or sponsorship (e.g. 'Council').

    — words which imply business pre-eminence or representative status (e.g. 'Association', 'Institute')

    — words which imply specific objects or functions ('Insurance', 'Trust', 'Fund'). It should be noted that the word 'co-operative' is one such word, but co-operatives using Model constitutions will normally be automatically allowed to use it

    — words for which permission must be obtained from a relevant body (e.g. to use the words 'Health Centre' permission must be obtained from the Department of Health and Social Security)

    — words covered by specific legislation (e.g. the words 'Credit Union' are covered by the Credit Union Act 1979 and permission to use them must be obtained from the Registrar of Friendly Societies).

If in doubt about the use of words in the co-ops name the reader is referred to **'Notes for Guidance - Company Names'**, a free leaflet from the Registrar of Companies (ref. C57). You should be able to consult a copy at your local reference library or Co-operative Development Agency. See also the **ICOM Factsheet: 'Choosing a Name for your Co-operative'**.

As well as being concerned that you don't inadvertently use a name which another organization is already using you need to be on the look out for anyone else using your name. You can sue another person who is using the same or a similar name if you can prove that they are damaging your trade because of that use. If your name is of particular importance it can be registered as a trade mark on goods or a service mark. Further information is available from **ICOM**.

To change the name of your co-perative the procedures are as follows. The stages to go through for a *co-operative company* are:

- decide on the new name and check that it is suitable for use in line with the information given above
- the name must be changed by a *special resolution* at a *general meeting* and record this in the minutes book. The special resolution must be passed by a three-quarters majority of members present in person and voting — unless your constitution says otherwise. Send a copy of the resolution to the **Registrar of Companies** with a remittance of £40. Note that the change of name is not

No. of Company *123456789*

THE COMPANIES ACT 1985
COMPANY LIMITED BY GUARANTEE
~~ORDINARY~~/SPECIAL RESOLUTION
OF

XYLOPHONE CO-OPERATIVE limited

Passed the **4TH** day of **APRIL** 19**88**

At an ~~ordinary~~/extraordinary general meeting of the above
named Company, duly convened and held at:

49 HILL END, BARSLOW

on the **4TH** day of **APRIL** 19**88**
The following resolution~~(s)~~ was/~~were~~ duly passed:

*THAT THIS COMPANY CHANGED ITS NAME TO
BARSLOW MUSIC CO-OPERATIVE LIMITED.*

signed *Jane Bell*
~~director or~~ secretary
of Company

date *4/4/88*

Specimen special resolution to change the name of the co-operative
— Co-operative company

effective until a certificate of incorporation on change of name is sent back
by the Registrar
- make the necessary changes to letterheads and other *stationery*; change the
name displayed outside registered office and order a new *common seal*
- inform your bank, all suppliers and all other people dealing with your
business. It is as well to tell them that the business has only changed its name
but not changed in any other respect.

A specimen special resolution for a co-operative company is given on page 65.

The stages to go through for changing the name of a *co-operative society* are:
- decide on a new name and check that it is suitable for use as above
- write to the **Registrar of Friendly Societies** to get preliminary approval — it is
always best to communicate with the Registrar at the earliest possible stage
to avoid problems later
- the name must be changed by passing a *special resolution* to that effect at
a *general meeting*. The resolution may be passed by a simple majority of
members present in person and voting — unless the rules say otherwise
- notify the registrar using Form C (see specimen on page 67)
- the Registrar will acknowledge the change of name on Form K but you should
note that the change is not effective until registered
- make the necessary changes to your rules and issue new copies as
appropriate. Change your letterheads and other *stationery*, change the name
displayed outside the registered office, order a new *common seal*
- inform your bank, all suppliers and all other people dealing with your
business pointing out that the business has only changed its name but not in
any other respect.

In addition to your co-operative's registered name you can use a business name.
If you do this the legal requirement is that when you use the business name on
your *stationery* that you also state that the business is owned by your co-op and
give its official registered name, registered number and registered office address.
So for example a co-operative called 'Drayton Parslow Workers Co-operative
Limited' could trade under the name of 'Paragon Press'. You should make sure that
your business name is not similar to one someone else is using, or they can sue
for 'passing off' (pretending that you are connected with them). Any sensitive words
in your proposed business name should be approved by the **Department of Trade
and Industry**.

FEE PAYABLE. See F. 823 Form C

INDUSTRIAL AND PROVIDENT SOCIETIES ACT 1965

Application for Approval of Change of Name pursuant to Section 5 of the Act

Name already
registered XYLOPHONE CO-OPERATIVE Limited

Register No. 123456 R

To the Chief Registrar (or Assistant Registrar for Scotland where the society is registered and does business exclusively in Scotland).

1. By a resolution passed at a general meeting of the society held on 4TH APRIL 1988 of which notice of the intention to propose the resolution was duly given in accordance with section 5 of the said Act it was resolved that the name of the society be changed to BARSLOW MUSIC CO-OPERATIVE Limited.

2. Application is hereby made for approval of the said change of name.

Signed on behalf of the Society

Jane Bell

Secretary

Date 4.4.88

Bas 89972/8306791 1m 4/82 P

Form C — Application for Approval of Change of Name — Co-operative society — *(source Registrar of Friendly Societies)*

Changing the constitution

Making a change to the legal constitution (the *rules* or the *memorandum and articles*) of a co-operative is a matter which needs very careful consideration. Very occasionally co-ops need to change their constitutions to bring them up to date or make small technical changes.

For example a co-operative using an old Model rules constitution may wish to change its rules to a new, revised Model. Or a co-operative society may consider that the restriction on the maximum amount of borrowing allowed by its rules has been eroded by inflation over a period of time and therefore wish to increase that figure.

Co-ops are advised to seek advice before going too far down the road of considering changes which may or may not be sound from a legal point of view. Another factor to consider is the cost of making the changes. Once the proposed changes have been properly considered and advice taken then the procedures are as follows:

Co-operative company

- make the proposed changes the subject of a *special resolution* at an *extraordinary general meeting* (EGM)
- call the EGM and pass the resolution by a 75% majority of those members present in person — otherwise the resolution fails
- if the resolution is agreed send a copy of it to the Registrar of Companies within 15 days together with a copy of the amended *memorandum and articles*. No fee is payable to the Registrar
- issue amended copies of the memorandum and articles to members, the bank, the auditors and the management committee
- the change is valid from the time of the EGM — unless subsequently challenged through the courts.

Co-operative society

- discuss the proposed change to the rules with the Registrar of Friendly Societies by telephone and letter. You are strongly advised to do this as the Registrar may otherwise reject the proposed amendment
- make the proposed changes the subject of a *special resolution* at an *extraordinary general meeting* (EGM)
- call the EGM and pass the resolution by a 75% majority of those members present in person — otherwise the resolution fails

- send the amended rules to Registrar for registration along with the fee they direct
- await registration which may take several weeks. The amendment is not valid until Registration has been completed
- issue amended copies of the memorandum and articles to members, the bank, the auditors, and the management committee.

Changing the objects of a co-operative

A co-operative may change the nature of its operations or its form of business and, following this, consider that the *objects clauses* in its constitution do not properly cover these new operations. In this case the co-operative could find itself trading *ultra-vires* (outside of its powers). There are serious consequences resulting from ultra-vires trading and the members of the co-operative, especially those who are members of the management committee, could lose their limited liability protection. To avoid this problem the co-operative may wish to amend its objects. In this type of case it is essential for the co-op to get legal advice. Talk to ICOM, your local Co-operative Development Agency or lawyer before taking any action.

Changing the auditors of a co-operative

If a co-operative decides that it wants to change its *auditors* this change normally takes place at the annual *general meeting* (AGM). An agenda item would be tabled at the AGM to appoint the new auditor and if the item were passed by the meeting they would be appointed. Notices of the AGM should be sent to both auditors (old and new). The secretary or treasurer of the co-op should then write to the old and new auditors explaining the position.

Creditors and others may be wary when there is a change in auditor for no apparent reason. So change only when you have good reason to do so and if necessary notify interested parties, for example your bank, of those reasons.

An auditor normally holds office from one AGM to the next. However if the management committee wish to remove the auditor before the end of their term they may do so by calling a *general meeting* and tabling a resolution asking for the auditor to be removed. (A co-op company should inform the Registrar of Companies on Form 386.) The auditor has a right to receive a notice of the meeting, to attend it and to be heard at it. An auditor removed from office in this way also has a right to attend the general meeting when their term of office would have normally expired, and also the general meeting when their successor is to be appointed. They have the right to receive notices of and be heard at those meetings as well.

In the event of a 'casual vacancy', when an auditor retires before the end of the term of office, the management committee (co-operative company) or general meeting (co-operative society) may appoint a successor.

Exceptionally an auditor may resign "under circumstances which the auditor considers should be brought to the attention of the members and/or creditors of the co-operative". In this case the auditor will send a statement, which must not be defamatory, of these circumstances to the co-op. The secretary of a company co-op should send a copy of the notice to the Registrar of Companies within 14 days as well as copies to all members and debenture holders. The auditor may also requisition an *extraordinary general meeting* (EGM) to consider that matter. The co-op is strongly advised to take legal advice under these circumstances.

Section 5

If the worst should happen

This section deals with issues relating to when a co-operative ceases trading or becomes insolvent. It is hoped that your co-operative will never need to use most of this information, but it is here to help you deal these matters if they occur.

The section covers:
- how to wind up a co-operative when it ceases trading
- what do do if the co-operative becomes insolvent
- how the members of the management committee may become personally liable for the debts of the co-operative, or may be disqualified from holding office.

Winding up the co-operative

These notes on winding up are a brief summary of the matters to be dealt with if it is decided that your co-operative should cease trading. There are penalties for not complying with the law during winding up. In most cases advice on correct procedures should be sought from your usual adviser — ICOM, your local Co-operative Development Agency, your accountant or lawyer.

A co-operative is technically insolvent when it cannot pay its bills as and when they become due for payment. Any co-operators considering that they are in, or approaching, this position should seek advice at once from their auditor or accountant. If they are subsequently advised to cease trading they should do so immediately and not make any payments to creditors until it is clear whether or not the co-op is actually solvent.

Whether the co-op will actually be liquidated or not will depend on whether there are sufficient funds left in the business to pay for the costs of liquidation. If funds are available an authorized insolvency practitioner will be appointed to a co-operative company who will wind up the co-operative in accordance with the Insolvency Act 1985. There is a special, simple procedure for solvent co-operative societies.

The types of winding up are:

Voluntary arrangements
In this type of winding up the co-op comes to an agreement with its creditors about how much each will receive. This method will work only with the agreement of all parties and is called a 'composition' or 'scheme of arrangement'.

Administration orders
In this arrangement an administrator, who must be a qualified insolvency

practitioner, will attempt to sell the business as a going concern so that the debts of the business can be paid. The administrator must get the agreement of the creditors to do this.

Receivers and managers

The debenture holders may appoint an administrative receiver (who must be a qualified insolvency practitioner). The job of the receiver is to realize — sell off — the assets of the business in order principally to pay the debenture holders and preferential creditors. Any surplus funds would be used to pay other creditors.

Winding up by the court

The court may appoint the official receiver or a liquidator to wind up the co-op. The receiver or liquidator will realize the assets of the business and pay the creditors as far as possible. If there are insufficient funds to pay for the costs of winding up the Registrar may dissolve the co-op.

Members' or creditors' voluntary winding up

If a co-operative chooses to wind up voluntarily it does so either as a 'members voluntary winding up', if it is solvent, or as a 'creditors voluntary winding up', if it is insolvent.

In a members voluntary winding up the directors (management committee) of the co-operative must make a 'declaration of solvency' which is a statutory declaration that the co-operative will be able to pay all of its debts within a period of twelve months.

During a winding up process care must be taken not to give preferential treatment to any one creditor over another. Indeed any transaction made by a co-op within a period of two years prior to the commencement of winding up may be treated as a 'fraudulent preference' and may be invalid and the creditor have to repay it.

During a winding up process all the co-op's correspondence to outside parties should indicate that the co-op is in the process of being wound up.

Ranking of debts in insolvent liquidation

When a co-op is wound up and is insolvent the debts are ranked by law in preferential order so that those with highest preference are paid first and any residue used to pay the next rank and so on.

The first debts to be paid off are debts secured against specific assets, for example debts which are secured by debentures which are fixed charges.

The second rank of creditors consist of the following paid in this order:

> PAYE (up to one year's worth)
> subcontract tax (tax deducted from payments made to subcontractors)
> VAT (up to six month's worth)
> car tax (up to one year's worth)
> betting and gaming duty (up to one year's worth)
> National Insurance contributions (up to one year's worth)
> pension contributions
> wages (up to four month's worth, or a maximum of £800 for each
>   employee, whichever is the less)
> accrued holiday pay to employees
> payments in respect of reserve forces.

The third rank of payments to be made are to holders of debentures which are floating charges.

Ranked fourth are payments to unsecured creditors. This category includes repayment of unsecured loans made by co-op members to the co-op.

In the event of there being insufficient funds to pay all debts in a particular category then proportional payments are made.

If the co-op is insolvent and unable to pay wages owed to employees, they are able to make a claim to the state redundancy fund.

Contributions by members to debts and liabilities

Members of a co-op are protected by limited liability from having to contribute to the debts and liabilities of the co-op during winding up — unless the co-op has been involved in *wrongful or fraudulent trading* in which case management committee members may be liable. However, members of co-op companies (who were members up to a year prior to winding up) will have to contribute the amount of their guarantees (normally £1 each).

Simple types of winding up when solvent

This section describes simple methods of winding up when a co-op has ceased trading and is solvent, that is it is able to meet all of its debts. When a co-op ceases trading and is insolvent it is recommended that the co-op seeks professional advice.

There are different procedures for co-op societies and co-op companies:

Co-operative society

First of all it must be asked is the society actually solvent? If it is only slightly insolvent, can it be made solvent by members making a small contribution, or by negotiating with creditors? If 'yes' to either of these questions, proceed through the following steps, otherwise abandon this procedure and seek advice.

- check the dissolution clause of your co-op's *constitution*. Call a meeting of members and get them to agree about disposal of the assets and that the society's registration be cancelled. If you can't call a meeting get each member to sign a standard letter to this effect
- when you are absolutely certain that the society is solvent, liquidate all assets and pay all debts
- earmark some of the remaining funds for winding up expenses (including paying the person doing the work). Distribute the remaining funds as previously agreed
- draw up final accounts for the co-operative since the last *annual return*. There is no need for an audit
- obtain Form L from the Registrar of Friendly Societies
- obtain a quote from a local newspaper for the standard advertisement (see reverse of Form L)
- complete Form L and return it to the Registrar along with: a statement declaring that the society has no assets or liabilities; the standard fee and the cost of the advertisement; a copy of the final accounts
- the Registrar will place the advert and confirm cancellation of the Registration of the society.

If there is the remotest possibility that the company might either be insolvent or become insolvent during the process described above, for example due to assets not realising as much as was thought, then the procedure must not be used. Instead a creditors' voluntary winding up is probably appropriate. Take advice if you think that this is a likely situation.

Co-operative company

The procedure for cancellation of registration is as follows:

- ensure that the co-op company is solvent or can be made solvent as described for a co-operative society above
- check the dissolution clause of your co-op's constitution. Call a meeting of members and get them to agree about disposal of any remaining assets and to dissolve the co-operative
- when you are absolutely certain that the co-operative is solvent, liquidate all assets and pay all debts. Retain a balance for winding up expenses and distribute remaining funds as previously agreed

- write to the registrar requesting cancellation of registration of the co-operative company under Section 652 of the **Companies Act 1985**. The Registrar will want assurances that the co-operative has no assets or liabilities and is no longer carrying on a business or is in operation.

If there is the remotest possibility that the company might either be insolvent or become insolvent during the process described above, for example due to assets not realising as much as was thought, then the procedure must not be used and instead a creditors' voluntary winding up is probably appropriate. Take advice if you think that this is a likely situation.

It is a serious offence to wind up a company as solvent when this is not the case.

Common ownership of assets

If your co-op has an ICOM model constitution you will find that its dissolution clause prohibits the distribution of residual assets to members at the time of winding up. This is because those assets are the results of the work of all the members of the co-op, not just the members at the time the co-op ceased trading.

For common ownership co-ops the remaining money or other assets may be used to support other co-operatives — by direct finance or through funding and support agencies such as **ICOM** and **ICOF** — or the money can be used for charitable purposes.

Wrongful/fraudulent trading

The definition of 'wrongful trading' is allowing a business to continue trading when you know that there is no reasonable prospect that insolvent liquidation can be avoided. The members of the *management committee* of a co-op should ensure at all times to the best of their ability that the co-op is not insolvent.

If the members of a management committee allow a co-op to continue trading when they know it to be insolvent they risk losing their personal limited liability and may be required to make a contribution to the debts and liabilities of the co-op.

To safeguard themselves the members of a management committee should seek urgent professional advice if they suspect that their co-op may be insolvent. If they are advised to cease trading they should take immediate steps to do so.

Fraudulent training occurs if a co-op carries on business with an intent to defraud creditors (or for any other fraudulent purpose). Any person knowingly being a party to this is liable to a fine or imprisonment or both.

Disqualification of management committee members

Any person who is a member of the management committee of a co-op which became insolvent as a result of that person's actions (in the opinion of a liquidator) could be disqualified by the court from being the director of a company or member of the management committee of a co-op. The period of disqualification may be up to fifteen years.

Conclusion

This is the end of the book, only the appendices follow. At this point you should have a good idea about most of the things that the secretary of a co-operative has to deal with.

Most of the work is simple and straightforward and you should now be able to carry it out yourself without assistance.

But some things are more obscure and in dealing with these matters and indeed whenever you are unsure - seek advice. Help is available from many sources and I repeat the usual list once again. Get help from ICOM, your local Co-operative Development Agency, your accountant or lawyer. Above all do not worry, someone is sure to know the solution to your problem!

Good Luck!

Information

Books and Legislation

Many co-operatives will find that they can carry out their secretarial duties without much need to refer to other books. If you want to refer to the actual legislation then it is often better to buy a book which includes the relevant acts and comments on them rather than trying to look through the legislation itself. Co-operative societies are strongly recommended to refer to CJ Chappenden's book (see below) if they require additional information. Co-operative companies should obtain copies of any appropriate notes from the Registrar of Companies, particularly *Notes for guidance of registered companies* (see below). For additional information refer to the list of books dealing with Company Law, bearing in mind that these are are a small selection of the large number available.

Company Law

AL Chapman and RM Ballard (eds), *Tolley's Company Law* (2nd Edition 1988, ISBN 0 85459 2598). Reference book.

John H Farrar, *Company Law* (Butterworth, 1985, ISBN 0 406 58161 4). Reference book.

Keith Walmsley (ed), *Butterworth's Company Law Handbook* (6th Edition 1987, ISBN 0 406 14315 3). A guide to the Companies Acts with notes.

Notes for guidance available from Companies Registration Office (generally free of charge):
> *Incorporation of new companies*, Ref: C56
> *Notes for guidance of registered companies*, Ref: NG1
> *A guide for Public Search*, Ref: C56e
> *Company names*, Ref: C57
> *Obligation to print certain documents*, Ref: C288
> *Accounting reference date*, Ref: GEN110
> *Disclosure of business ownership/Control of business names*, Ref: NG2
> *Disclosure of company accounts — small, medium and dormant companies*, Ref: C478
> *Companies wishing to be exempt from requirement to use the word limited in the company name*, Ref: C481
> *General Brief*, Ref: C483
> *Sensitive words and expressions — company and business names*, Ref: C499
> *Disclosure requirements*, Ref: C505
> *Specimen ordinary/special resolution*, Ref: CAP21
> *Specimen special resolution on change of name*, Ref: NC19

Specimen written resolution, Ref: NC20
Companies records: supply of copies by post, Ref: PN1

(a complete list of forms and notes available, of which the above is an abbreviated list, is available from the Companies Registration Office, Ref: STA8)

Co-operative Law

CJ Chappenden, *Handbook to the Industrial and Provident Societies Act 1965* (Co-operative Union, 1965, supplements 1970 & 1980, ISBN 0 85195 124 4). A complete guide to the legislation including copies of the act.

Ian Snaith, *The Law of Co-operatives* (Waterlow, 1984, ISBN 0 08 039159 1). Reference book.

Notes from the Registrar of Friendly Societies (generally free of charge):
Registration of co-operative societies, Ref: F617. Includes notes about the definition of bona fide co-operative societies.
List of Fees Payable, Ref: F823

see also:
ICOM factsheet: Choosing a name for your co-operative, available from ICOM

Legislation

(some of the books given above contain a copy of the relevant legislation)
Business Names Act 1985
Companies Act 1985
Insolvency Act 1985
Industrial Common Ownership Act 1976 — this Act is not mentioned in the text of this book, however it does contain useful legal definitions of co-operative and common ownership enterprises.

Laws applying to Co-operative Societies only:
Industrial and Provident Societies Act 1965
Industrial and Provident Societies Act 1967
The Friendly and Industrial and Provident Societies Act 1968
Industrial and Provident Societies Act 1975
Industrial and Provident Societies Act 1978

Copies of all legislation available from Her Majesty's Stationery Office.

Running a Co-operative

Peter Cockerton and Anna Whyatt, *The Workers Co-operative Handbook* (ICOM Co-Publications, ISBN 0 946776 10 5)

John Berry and Mark Roberts, *Co-op Management and Employment* (ICOM Co-Publications, ISBN 0 946776 04 0)

Richard Macfarlane, *Financial Planning and Control* (ICOM Co-Publications, ISBN 0 946776 08 3)

Gerry Finnegan, *Marketing for Co-ops* (ICOM Co-Publications, ISBN 0 946776 06 7)

ICOM Legal Working Party, *Model Employment Contract for Worker Co-operatives* (ICOM Co-Publications, ISBN 0 946776 09 1)

Malcolm Lynch, *ICOM Finance Pack* (ICOM Co-Publications, August 1988, ISBN 0 946776 14 8)

General Reference Books

Croner's reference book for the self employed and smaller business, (Croner Publications)

Croner's reference book for employers, (Croner Publications)

Larger co-ops may also be interested in *Croner's Employment Law.*

Equal opportunities

Code of practice for the elimination of racial discrimination and the promotion of opportunities in employment, (Commission for Racial Equality)

Code of Practice for the elimination of discrimination on the grounds of sex and marriage and the promotion of equality of opportunity in employment, (Equal Opportunities Commission)

Code of Practice on the employment of disabled people, (Manpower Services Commission)

Useful Addresses

National

INDUSTRIAL COMMON OWNERSHIP MOVEMENT (ICOM)
THE NATIONAL FEDERATION OR
WORKER CO-OPERATIVES
VASSALLI HOUSE
20 CENTRAL ROAD
LEEDS
LS1 6DE
0532 467138/7

LONDON ICOM
8 BRADBURY STREET
LONDON
N16 8JN
01 249 2837

ICOM WOMEN'S LINK-UP
VASSALLI HOUSE
20 CENTRAL ROAD
LEEDS
LS1 6DE
0532 467138

CO-OPERATIVE DEVELOPMENT AGENCY (NATIONAL)
BROADMEAD HOUSE
21 PANTON STREET
LONDON
SW1Y 4DR
01 839 2987

and at:
HOLYOAKE HOUSE
HANOVER STREET
MANCHESTER
M60 0AS
061 833 9379

CO-OPERATIVE BANK PLC
PO BOX 101
BALLON STREET
MANCHESTER
M60 4EP
061 829 4280

INDUSTRIAL COMMON OWNERSHIP FINANCE (ICOF)
4 ST GILES STREET
NORTHAMPTON
NN1 1AA
O604 37563

Training and Consultancy

CO-OPERATIVE ADVISORY GROUP
ANTONIA HOUSE
262 HOLLOWAY ROAD
LONDON
N7 6NE
01 609 7017/8

CO-OPERATIVE BUSINESS SYSTEMS
12 MOSLEY STREET
MANCHESTER
M2 3AQ
061 236 1493

COUNTERPOINT MANAGEMENT SERVICES
76 BANKSIDE STREET
LEEDS
LS8 5AD
0532 402981

and at:
82C EARLHAM GROVE
LONDON
E7 9AZ
01 555 0153

KIRKLEES COMMUNITY ENTERPRISE TRAINING AGENCY
25 QUEENSGATE
HUDDERSFIELD
YORKSHIRE
0484 516067

LONDON CO-OPERATIVE TRAINING
    5 BRADBURY STREET
    LONDON N16 8JN
    01 254 7051

LYNXS WOMENS TRAINING
    INTERNATIONAL COMMUNITY
    CENTRE
    61B MANSFIELD ROAD
    NOTTINGHAM
    NG1 3FN
    0602 473010

MARKETING RESOURCE CENTRE
    11/13 CHARTERHOUSE BUILDINGS
    LONDON
    EC1M 7AN
    01 608 1144

NEW WORKING WOMEN
    14 ST GEORGE STREET
    LEEDS
    LS1
    0532 432474

SPECTRUM
    SUITE 319
    SOUTH BANK HOUSE
    BLACK PRINCE ROAD
    LONDON
    SE1 7SJ
    01 582 9191

Academic

CO-OPERATIVE COLLEGE
    STANFORD HALL
    LOUGHBOROUGH
    LEICESTER
    LE12 5QR
    050 982 2333

CO-OPERATIVES RESEARCH UNIT
    SYSTEMS GROUP

OPEN UNIVERSITY
WALTON HALL
MILTON KEYNES
MK7 6AA
0908 652102/3

Official Bodies

COMMISSION FOR RACIAL EQUALITY
    ELLIOT HOUSE
    10-12 ALLINGTON STREET
    LONDON SW1E 5EH

DEPARTMENT OF EMPLOYMENT:
SMALL FIRMS SERVICE
    STEEL HOUSE
    TOTHILL STREET
    LONDON
    SW1H 9NF
    DIAL 100, FREEPHONE ENTERPRISE

DEPARTMENT OF TRADE & INDUSTRY
    1-19 VICTORIA STREET
    LONDON
    SW1 H0ET
    01 215 7877

EQUAL OPPORTUNITIES COMMISSION
    OVERSEAS HOUSE
    QUAY STREET
    MANCHESTER
    M3 3HN

MANPOWER SERVICES COMMISSION
    MOORFOOT
    SHEFFIELD
    S1 4PQ
    0742 753275

REGISTRY OF FRIENDLY SOCIETIES
    15/17 GREAT MARLBOROUGH
    STREET
    LONDON W1V 2AX
    01 437 9992

and at:
58 FREDERICK STREET
EDINBURGH
EH2 1NB
031 226 3224

and at:
43-47 CHICHESTER STREET
BELFAST
BT1 4RJ
0232 234488

REGISTRAR OF COMPANIES
COMPANIES HOUSE
CROWN WAY
MAINDY
CARDIFF
CF4 3UZ
0222 388588

and at:
102 GEORGE STREET
EDINBURGH
EH2 3DJ
031 225 5774

and at:
43-47 CHICHESTER STREET
BELFAST
BT1 4RJ
0232 34121

Regional support

DERBYSHIRE ENTERPRISE BOARD
95 SHEFFIELD ROAD
CHESTERFIELD
DERBYSHIRE
S41 7JH
0246 207390

GREATER LONDON ENTERPRISE
63-67 NEWINGTON CAUSEWAY
LONDON
SE1 6BD
01 403 0300

**HIGHLANDS AND ISLANDS
DEVELOPMENT BOARD**
BRIDGE HOUSE
27 BANK STREET
INVERNESS
IV1 1QR
0463 234171

LANCASHIRE ENTERPRISES LTD
LANCASHIRE HOUSE
WATERY LANE
PRESTON
LANCASHIRE
PR2 2XE
0772 735821

**LONDON CO-OPERATIVE ENTERPRISE
BOARD**
11-13 CHARTERHOUSE BUILDINGS
LONDON
EC1M 7AN
01 608 1141/2/3

MERSEYSIDE ENTERPRISE BOARD
ROYAL LIVER BUILDING
WATER STREET
LIVERPOOL
L3 1HT
051 236 0221

**WEST MIDLANDS CO-OPERATIVE
FINANCE LTD**
31/34 WATERLOO STREET
BRIMINGHAM
B2 5TJ
021 236 2708

**WEST YORKSHIRE SMALL FIRMS FUND
LTD**
GROUND FLOOR
KERSHAW HOUSE
55 WELL STREET
BRADFORD
BD1 5PS
0274 754546

Local Co-operative Development Agencies

ANTUR TEIFI
CRAIG CHAMBERS
NEWCASTLE EMLYN
DYFED
WALES
SA38 9DA
0239 710238

ASHINGTON COMMUNITY INITIATIVES CENTRE
STATION VILLA
KENILWORTH ROAD
ASHINGTON
NORTHUMBERLAND
NE63 9XL
0670 853619

AVON CDA
108A STOKES CROFT
BRISTOL
AVON
BS1 3RU
0272 428853

BARNSLEY ENTERPRISE CENTRE
1 PONTEFRACT ROAD
BARNSLEY
SOUTH YORKSHIRE
S71 1AJ
0226 298091

BASILDON DISTRICT CDA
UNIT 27
CORNAWALLIS HOUSE
HOWARDS CHASE
BASILDON
ESSEX
SS14 1BB
0268 282171/282187

BEDFORDSHIRE AND DISTRICT CDA
TAVISTOCK HOUSE

34 BROMHAM ROAD
BEDFORD
MK40 20D
0234 213571

BIRMINGHAM EMPLOYMENT INITATIVE UNIT
136 DIGBETH
BIRMINGHAM
B5 6DR
021 643 4343

BIRMINGHAM CDA
ZAIR WORKS
CO-OPERATIVE ENTERPRISE CENTRE
111-119 BISHOP STREET
BIRMINGHAM
B5 6JL
021 643 3531

BLACK COUNTRY CDA
LICH CHAMBERS
EXCHANGE STREET
WOLVERHAMPTON
WEST MIDLANDS
WV1 1TS
0902 312736

BOLTON NEIGHBOURHOOD ECONOMIC DEVELOPMENT AGENCY
LINCOLN MILL
WASHINGTON STREET
BOLTON
LANCASHIRE
BL3 5EY
0204 22213

BRENT CDA
192 HIGH ROAD
WILLESDEN
LONDON
NW10 2PB
01 451 3777

BRIGHTON AREA CDA

85 LONDON ROAD
BRIGHTON
E.SUSSEX
BN1 4JF
0273 606722 X 7

CAMBRIDGE CDA
THE BUSINESS ADVICE CENTRE
71A LENSFIELD ROAD
CAMBRIDGE
CB2 1EN
0223 60977

**CAMDEN CO-OPERATIVE
DEVELOPMENT OFFICER**
ECONOMIC DEVELOPMENT UNIT
TOWN HALL
EUSTON ROAD
LONDON NW1 2RU
01 278 4444

CAMDEN ENTERPRISE AGENCY
57 PRATT STREET
CAMDEN
LONDON
NW1 0DP
01 482 2128

CARDIFF & VALE CDA
ENTERPRISE HOUSE
127 BUTE STREET
CARDIFF
WALES
CF1 5EL
0222 494411

CENTRAL LONDON CDA
THE KIDS BUILDING
80 WAYNFLETE SQUARE
LONDON
W10 6UH
01 968 7744

CDS TRAINING FOR ENTERPRISE
41 BOLD STREET
LIVERPOOL

L1 4EU
051 708 0674

CHESHIRE (NORTH) CDA
UNIT 3
CATHERINE STREET
BEWSEY INDUSTRIAL ESTATE
WARRINGTON
WA5 5LH
0925 35158

CLEVELAND CDA
10A ALBERT ROAD
MIDDLESBROUGH
CLEVELAND
TS1 1QA
0642 210224

COLCHESTER CDA
2 COLVIN CLOSE
COLCHESTER
ESSEX
C03 4BS
0206 67793

COVENTRY CDA
UNIT 15
THE ARCHES INDUSTRIAL ESTATE
SPON END
COVENTRY
CV1 3JQ
0203 714078

CROYDON CDA
34A STATION ROAD
WEST CROYDON
SURREY
CR0 2RB
01 686 1966

DELYN CDA
BRYN MYWION BACH
LLANARMON YN IAL
MOLD
CLWYD
08243 728

DERBYSHIRE CDA
SUN ALLIANCE HOUSE
CURZON STREET
DERBY
DERBYSHIRE
DE1 1LL
0332 380515

DEVON CDA
EXETER WORKSHOPS
39 MARSH GREEN ROAD
MARSH BARTON
EXETER
EX2 8PN
0392 72223

DURHAM COUNTY COUNCIL
INDUSTRIAL BUREAU
PLANNING DEPARTMENT
COUNTY HALL
DURHAM
DH1
0385 64411 x2365

EALING CDA
CHARLES HOUSE
BRIDGE ROAD
SOUTHALL
MIDDLESEX
UB2 4BD
01 574 4724

EAST ANGLIA CDA
THE GLASS HOUSE
WENSUM STREET
NORWICH
NR3 1LA
051 708 0674

EDINBURGH CDA
137 BUCCLEUGH STREET
EDINBURGH
EH8 9NE

EDINBURGH DISTRICT COUNCIL
ECONOMIC DEVELOPMENT &

ESTATES DEPARTMENT
375 HIGH STREET
EDINBURGH
EH1 1QE
031 225 2424 X5807

ENFIELD CDA
CO-OP HALL
444 HERTFORD ROAD
ENFIELD
EN3 5QH
01 805 7950

ESSEX CDA
CHELMER COURT
CHURCH STREET
CHELMSFORD
ESSEX
CM1 1NH
0245 350388

**GLASTONBURY CO-OPERATIVE
DEVELOPMENT GROUP**
C/O ASSEMBLEY ROOMS
GLASTONBURY
SOMERSET

GLOUCESTER CDA
SHIRE HALL
WESTGATE STREET
GLOUCESTER
GL1 2TG
0454 425093

GREAT YARMOUTH CDA
QUEENS ROAD BUSINESS CENTRE
QUEENS ROAD
GREAT YARMOUTH
NR30 3HT
0493 857 648

**GREENWICH EMPLOYMENT RESOURCE
UNIT**
311 PLUMSTEAD HIGH ROAD
PLUMSTEAD
LONDON

SE18 1JX
01 310 6695/6

HACKNEY CO-OP DEVELOPMENTS
16 DALSTON LANE
HACKNEY
LONDON
E8 3AZ
01 254 4829

**HAMMERSMITH & FULHAM
COMMUNITY ENTERPRISE**
PALINGSWICK HOUSE
241 KING STREET
LONDON
W6 9LP
01 741 2304

HAMPSHIRE CDA
130 FRANCIS AVENUE
SOUTHSEA
PORTSMOUTH
HANTS
0705 822211

**HARINGEY ECONOMIC DEVELOPMENT
UNIT**
LONDON BOROUGH OF HARINGEY
72 LAWRENCE ROAD
LONDON N15 4EG
01 802 3191

HARLOW CDA
LOTTON BUSH CENTRE
SOUTHERN WAY
HARLOW
ESSEX
CM18 7BL
0279 446086

**HASTINGS CO-OPERATIVE
DEVELOPMENT UNIT**
HASTINGS BOROUGH COUNCIL
18 CORNWALLIS GARDENS
HASTINGS
EAST SUSSEX

TN34 1LP
0424 446529

HOUNSLOW CDA
30 HEATH ROAD
HOUNSLOW
MIDDLESEX
TW3 2NN

HUMBERSIDE CDA
1ST FLOOR
FERENSWAY CHAMBERS
79 FERENSWAY
HULL
HU2 8LD
0482 28160

and at:

7C COLIN ROAD
SCUNTHORPE
HUMBERSIDE
DN16 1TT
0724 850774

IPSWICH & SUFFOLK CDA
5 CANADA COTTAGES
LAVENHAM ROAD
LINDSEY
SUFFOLK
IP7 6PW

IPSWICH BOROUGH COUNCIL
EMPLOYMENT DEVELOPMENT
OFFICE
CIVIC CENTRE
CIVIC DRIVE
IPSWICH IP1 2EE
0473 211211

ISLINGTON CDA
177 UPPER STREET
LONDON
N1 1RG
01 226 2783

KALA UJAMAA LTD
SUITE 220
SOUTHBANK HOUSE
BLACK PRINCE ROAD
LONDON
SE1 7SJ
01 587 1634/0243

KENSINGTON BUSINESS RESOURCE CENTRE
CO-OPERATIVE DEVELOPMENT
WORKER
9 THORPE CLOSE
LONDON
W10 5XL
01 969 9455

KINGSTON AND RICHMOND CDA
58B LONDON ROAD
KINGSTON ON THAMES
SURREY
KT2 6QA
01-549 9159

KIRKLEES METROPOLITAN COUNCIL
ECONOMIC DEVELOPMENT UNIT
KIRKLEES HOUSE
MARKET STREET
HUDDERSFIELD
HD1 2EY
0484 22133

LAMBETH CDA
CO-OP CENTRE
11 MOWLL STREET
LONDON
SW9 6BE
01 582 0003

LANCASHIRE CDA
LANCASHIRE HOUSE
WATERY LANE
PRESTON LANCASHIRE
PR2 2XE
0772 723771

and at:
36 CHURCH STREET
BLACKBURN
LANCASHIRE
BB1 5AL
0254 388517

and at:
WHITECROSS MILL
WHITECROSS
LANCASTER
LA1 4XH
0254 390669

LATIN AMERICAN CO-OP DEVELOPMENT PROJECT (PLADECOOP)
11 MOWLL STREET
LONDON
SW9 6BG
01 582 4482

LEEDS CITY COUNCIL
CO-OP DEVELOPMENT OFFICER
HEADROW BUILDINGS
44 THE HEADROW
LEEDS
LS1 8EA
0532 463208

LEICESTER AND COUNTY CDA
BUSINESS ADVICE CENTRE
30 NEW WALK
LEICESTERSHIRE
LE1 6TF
0533 547837

LEWISHAM BUSINESS ADVICE CENTRE
CO-OP SECTION
225 LEWISHAM HIGH STREET
LONDON
SE13 6LY
01 852 9207

LLANELLI CDA
LLANELLI COMMUNITY SERVICES
CASTLE BUILDINGS

MURRAY STREET
LLANELLI
DYFED
05542 55949

MANCHESTER (GREATER) CDA
23 NEW MOUNT STREET
MANCHESTER
M4 4DE
061 833 9496

and at:
C/O ORIC
7 COMMERCIAL ROAD
OLDHAM
OII IDP
061 626 4130

MANCHESTER (CITY) CDA
MANCODA
12 MOSLEY STREET
MANCHESTER
M2 3AQ
061 236 1274

MERSEYSIDE ENTERPRISE BOARD
CO-OPERATIVE DEVELOPMENT
UNIT
ROYAL LIVER BUILDING
WATER STREET
LIVERPOOL
L3 1HT
051 236 0221

MILTON KEYNES CDA
LEVEL THREE
CIVIC OFFICES
1 SAXON GATE EAST
CENTRAL MILTON KEYNES
MK9 3HJ
0908-660375

NEWHAM CDA
ESSEX HOUSE
375-377 HIGH STREET
STRATFORD

LONDON
E15 4OZ
01 519 2377

NORFOLK AND NORWICH CDA
THE GLASS HOUSE
9-13 WENSUM STREET
NORWICH
NORFOLK
NR3 1LA
0603-615200

NORTHAMPTONSHIRE CDA
OFFICE 3
THE FIRE STATION
UPPER MOUNT
NORTHAMPTON
NN1 3DN
0604 24040

NORTHERN IRELAND CDA
CANADA HOUSE
22 NORTH STREET
BELFAST
BT1 1LA
0232 232755

NORTHERN REGION CO-OPERATIVES DEVELOPMENT ASSOCIATION
BOLBEC HALL
WESTGATE ROAD
NEWCASTLE UPON TYNE
NE1 1SE
091 261 0140

and at:
THE INDUSTRIAL BUREAU
COUNTY HALL
DURHAM
DH1
0385 64411

NOTTINGHAMSHIRE CDA
DUNKIRK ROAD
DUNKIRK
NOTTINGHAM

NG7 2PH
0602 705700

OXFORDSHIRE CDA
14B PARK END STREET
OXFORD
OXON
OX1 1HW
0865 790623

PLYMOUTH CDA
138 NORTH ROAD EAST
PLYMOUTH
PL4 6AQ
0752 23481

PORT TALBOT CDA
2ND FLOOR ROYAL BUILDINGS
TALBOT ROAD
PORT TALBOT
WEST GLAMORGAN
SA13 1DN
0639 895173

REDDITCH CDA
TOWN HALL
ALCESTER STREET
REDDITCH
WORCESTERSHIRE
B98 8AH
0527 64252

ROTHERAM ENTERPRISE AGENCY
2ND FLOOR
SAINTS BUILDING
21 CORPORATION STREET
ROTHERAM
009 382121

SALFORD CEDA
9 BROADWAY
SALFORD
MANCHESTER
M5 2TS
061 872 3838

SCOTTISH CO-OP DEVELOPMENT COMMITTEE
ABERDEEN BUSINESS CENTRE
WILLOWBANK HOUSE
WILLOWBANK ROAD
ABERDEEN
AB1 2YG
0224 593159

and at:
ROYAL BANK BUILDINGS
191 HIGH STREET
KIRCALDY
FIFE
0592 200866

and at:
TEMPLETON BUSINESS CENTRE
TEMPLETON STREET
BRIDGETON
GLASGOW
G40 1DA
041 554 3797

and at:
AULTNASKIACH HOUSE
CULDUTHEL ROAD
INVERNESS
IV2 4UB
0463 222464

SHEFFIELD CO-OP DEVELOPMENT GROUP
PALATINE CHAMBERS
22 PINSTONE STREET
SHEFFIELD
S1 2HN
0742 734563

SOMERSET CO-OP ENTERPRISE CENTRE
2ND FLOOR
52 CLARE STREET
BRIDGWATER
SOMERSET
0278 453000

SOMERSET EDU
COUNTY HALL
TAUNTON
SOMERSET
TA1 4DY
0823 55394

SOUTH EAST WALES CDA
5 MOUNTSTUART SQUARE
CARDIFF
SOUTH GLAMORGAN
CF1 6EE

SOUTHAMPTON CDA
56 HIGH STREET
SOUTHAMPTON
SO1 0NS
0703 223885

SOUTHWARK CDA
KENNINGTON WORKSHOP
42 BRAGANZA STREET
WALWORTH
LONDON
SE17 3RJ
01 735 6066

**SPITALFIELDS SMALL BUSINESS
ASSOCIATION LTD**
170 BRICK LANE
LONDON
E1 6RU
01 247 1892

STAFFORDSHIRE (NORTH) CDA
TOWN HALL
STOKE-ON-TRENT
STAFFS
ST4 1HH
0782 48241 x201

**STEVENAGE & NORTH HERTFORDSHIRE
CDA**
C/O SEARCH
SOUTHGATE
STEVENAGE

HERTFORDSHIRE
SG1 1HB
O438 31377

**SUNDERLAND COMMON OWNERSHIP
ENTERPRISE RESOURCE CENTRE**
(SCOERC)
44 MOWBRAY ROAD
HENDON
SUNDERLAND
TYNE & WEAR
SR2 8EL
091 5650476

SWINDON CDA
3 HARDING STREET
SWINDON
WILTSHIRE
SN1 5BZ
0793 511802

TELFORD CDA
9 TELFORD ROAD
DAWLEY ROAD
TELFORD
SHROPSHIRE

TOWER HAMLETS CDA
84 WHITEHORSE ROAD
WHITECHAPEL
LONDON
E1 0ND
01 791 0450

**WALES CO-OPERATIVE DEVELOPMENT
AND TRAINING CENTRE**
LLANDAFF COURT
FAIRWATER ROAD
CARDIFF CFS 2XD
0222 554955

and at:
MORFA HALL
CHURCH STREET
RHYL
CLWYD

LL18 3AB
0745 55336

and at:
24 BRIDGE STREET
LAMPETER
DYFED
SA48 7AB
0570 423107

and at:
ENTERPRISE CENTRE
MERTHYR TYDFIL INDUSTRIAL
PARK
PENTREBACH
MERTHYR TYDFIL
MID GLAMORGAN
CF48 4DR
0443 692233

and at:
COUNCIL OFFICES
BRON CASTELL
STRYD FAWR
BANGOR
GWYNEDD
LL57 1YU
0248 364 729

WALTHAM FOREST EDU
195 WOOD STREET
WALTHAMSTOW
LONDON
E17
01 527 5544

WANDSWORTH BUSINESS RESOURCE CENTRE
129-133 ARNDALE SHOPPING
CENTRE
WANDSWORTH
LONDON
SW18 4TF
01 720 7053

WAVENEY CDA
TOWN HALL
LOWERSTOFT
SUFFOLK
NR32 1HS
0502 62111

WEST GLAMORGAN COMMON OWNERSHIP
DEVELOPMENT AGENCY
10 ST. HELENS ROAD
SWANSEA
WEST GLAMORGAN
SA1 4AN
0792 53498

WIGAN CDA
24 SPENCER ROAD
WIGAN
GREATER MANCHESTER
WN1 2PW
0942 321934

WREKIN DISTRICT COUNCIL
EMPLOYMENT DEVELOPMENT
OFFICER
PO BOX 213
MALINSEE HOUSE
TELFORD
SHROPSHIRE
TF3 4LD
0952 505051

YORK CITY COUNCIL
EMPLOYMENT DEVELOPMENT
UNIT
5 ST LEONARDS PLACE
YORK
YO1 2EX
0904 59881

YORK ENTERPRISE CENTRE
1 DAVYGATE
YORK
YO1 2QE
0904 641401

Index

Company Secretary Service

for Worker Co-operatives

a complete package designed to assist with all of the legal and administrative requirements involved in being a company secretary

the package consists of:
- change of secretary
- change of directors
- change of name
- change of registered office
- updating register of members/directors (annually)
- amendments to memorandum and articles of association
- amendments to ICOM Employment Contract
- filing annual return
- filing change in financial year end
- notices and minutes of annual general meetings

annual subscription £99.00

for full details about this new service contact:
Industrial Common Ownership Movement Limited
The National Federation of Worker Co-operatives
Vassalli House, 20 Central Road, Leeds, LS1 6DE
(0532) 461737/8

Other ICOM Co-Publications

The Workers Co-operative Handbook

Peter Cockerton and Anna Whyatt
The comprehensive guide to all aspects of setting up a workers co-operative — how to assess skills you will need and the products and services you can offer, how to draw up a business plan and raise finance. Includes specimens of the different legal structures it is possible to adopt as well as a discussion of the position and role of co-ops within the UK economy.

Financial Planning and Control: A Practical Guide

Richard Macfarlane
This guide takes the reader through the financial procedures and bookkeeping techniques a co-op needs to survive. Using non-technical language it explains costing and pricing, budgets, cash flows, record keeping and dealing with VAT, PAYE and corporation tax.

Marketing for Co-ops: a practical guide

Gerry Finnegan
How a co-op can define its market and begin to work out an effective marketing strategy. This guide looks at market research, packaging, pricing, distribution, promotion and how to monitor the effect of all these.

Co-op Management and Employment

John Berry and Mark Roberts
A wealth of guidance and discussion about how a co-op should run itself, how members should be involved and meetings organised, how information can be shared, how the local community can participate and, crucially, the obligations of the co-op as an employer.

Model Employment Contract for Worker Co-operatives

ICOM Legal Working Party
A pack of materials that allows a co-operative to tailor an employment contract to their particular needs. Based on the practical experience of different co-ops and taking account of the development of employment law it will help the co-op not only meet its legal obligations but develop satisfying working arrangements for all its members.

All the above are available from:
Turnaround Distribution, 27 Horsell Road, London N5 1XL
A full catalogue of publications about co-operatives is available on request.